C000158053

OnBoard

ALL YOU NEED
TO KNOW ABOUT
STARTING OUT IN
WORK TODAY

CanSultancy

Congratulations!

We'd like to offer you tʰ
team here and hope ↿
nd the opportuniⁱ
art of our f
benⱸ

Alph
Keogh

OnBoard

First published in 2020 by

Panoma Press Ltd
48 St Vincent Drive, St Albans, Herts, AL1 5SJ, UK
info@panomapress.com
www.panomapress.com

Book layout by Neil Coe.

978-1-784529-08-6

The right of Alph Keogh to be identified as the author of this work has been asserted in accordance with sections 77 and 78 of the Copyright, Designs and Patents Act 1988.

A CIP catalogue record for this book is available from the British Library.

This book is available online and in bookstores.

Dedication

With love to Marie-Luise and Katharina who
inspire me every day

Acknowledgements

When your professional profile identifies you as a facilitator, speaker and coach, people often tend to think that you should possess more answers than questions. The exact opposite is true. It takes the right question or a timely nod to move an individual or group forward in their discussions and thinking. Having facilitated and coached two or three times per month over the past 25 years I can confirm that it's an astonishingly pertinent and privileged way to learn. None of this vicarious learning requires any special qualifications apart from an ability to create conversational space and synthesise discussions into something greater than the sum of their parts, thus creating change. This I have learned from the many people, from across a host of different industries and countries, with whom I have worked over the years. If this book is a testament to anything, then it's to all those people and the extraordinary power of open dialogue. Some of these people are listed below:

Amy Avergun, Sesame Baker, Simon Barclay, Patrick Boland, Joke Bunnens, Nicolai Christiansen-Vinge, Paul Ejiro-Okpurughre, Konrad Fassnacht, Tom Fumarelli, Alexander Grots, Katharina Keogh, Guy McDonnell, Monika Medlewska, Livia Musso, Isabel Ponsgens, Florian Rustler, Mike Skoropski, Thomas Sewerin, Theresia Tauber, Anny Tubbs.

Drawings by Erik Petri.

Contents

Introduction

There is no end of advice and support for a person entering or trying to advance in the workforce today. There's personal coaching, psychological profiling, other people's success stories and any number of steps-to-success infographics you care to count. All of this is available in giga and terabytes. It can be accessed through the phone in your pocket, the tablet on the coffee table or the PC on your desk. It's like drinking from the proverbial firehose. The move from having 30 minutes of career advice at school or college to being buried in an almost unavoidable avalanche of tips and recommendations has been swift and voluminous.

People have become categorised into Gen this, that or the other, and employer branders would have us believe that one group should be treated like this and the other like that. Is it really that complicated? Of course, there has been change in the world but have the basic principles of going to work changed that much? Are human beings of varying ages now so different from each other and to such an extent that we need to corral them into a myriad of sub-groups and then figure how to treat each one in some unique way? I don't believe so. And no worries, I won't be categorising you in any way here. Millennial – there, I have said it for the first and last time.

This book features stories, anecdotes and tips instead of theory, statistics and case studies. It's a down to earth, practical guide to understanding both organisations and the people you will meet there, and it's specifically designed to help you make a great start in the modern workplace.

This is what this book is about:

- Preparing yourself in a very practical way for the challenges of organisational life. Sharpening your self-awareness and deploying your professional strengths at work.

- Focusing on and optimising the key working relationships, especially that with your boss, which can make or break your first year at work.

- Engaging with colleagues and ensuring that you maintain your sense of personal independence and still be a great team player.

- Getting an overview of what the ubiquitous meetings in organisations look like in the reality of a busy working day and how to get the best out of them.

- Understanding the larger organisational issues like culture, change and organisational structures and what they mean for you and your effectiveness in the workplace.

- Staying optimistic and finding a sense of meaning, fun and fulfilment at work, instead of stress, overwork and burnout.

CHAPTER ONE

Me, Myself And I Are Going To Work

"First find yourself, so that you can find me."

Rumi

The advice to 'be yourself' is a phrase that has entered the language as a default reaction to someone agonising over their performance on a particularly important life event. A friend once told me that his own mother had told him to 'be himself' before he went for a vital job interview. This left him musing over the notion that if even his own mother was unsure of who he was being (if not himself) then the sheer level of pretence regarding self-presentation in society must be far greater than we had ever imagined.

The other side of this coin is the phrase 'Who do you think you are?'. This phrase offers at least as many challenges to the sense of self as the previous one. If 'be yourself' was meant to elevate you then this one was meant to remind you that individuality or even ambition is not always welcome. Of course, if we delve just a little into the history of human interaction, we find out that being free to be ourselves either modestly or in more grandiose terms is a relatively new concept.

For the greater part of our human existence we have lived in small communities where the social hierarchies bound us to those around us in defined relationships. We would have pretty much met the same people every day of our lives so there was neither the opportunity nor the pressure to be anyone different from who we were in that community. Even seeing yourself as an individual was a rare occurrence with mirrors only being available to the masses from the early 19th century. A selfie in those days may have had more in common with Snapchat, as seeing your image in a pool of water was a very temporary experience indeed.

Urbanisation brought people into the cities; London, for example, grew from having 60,000 inhabitants in 1550 to 350,000 one hundred years later. So, people had to adapt to meeting new people in new situations and so had to develop the art of self-presentation and being appropriate to different types of people and changing circumstances.

Aligning all your versions of yourself

These days the world has expanded exponentially across cyberspace. You can be anyone you want to be and even to people you will never meet in the flesh. All of your possible selves can be manifested across a variety of social media platforms, from Facebook to LinkedIn to Instagram and a thousand apps in between. The forces compelling you to be yourself, from mothers to HR managers and coaches like myself have been usurped by the endless scope and depth of cyberspace. So, if someone says 'be yourself' you can truthfully answer 'Which one?' and if someone asks 'Who do you think you are?' you can honestly present them with a selection from your range of pseudonyms, avatars or cyber personalities.

However, let's not forget that cyberspace is a mile wide and an inch deep. And having exhausted all the possibilities of who you might be in cyberspace it's vital to keep in mind that it's you with your face and your brilliant ideas and glorious imperfections and not your HD LinkedIn photo or hyped Facebook presence that will have to show up for both interviews and work.

The final and oldest 'self' aphorism I want to share with you is the ancient Greek – γνῶθι σεαυτό – translated as 'know thyself'. This was inscribed over the entrance to the temple of Apollo at Delphi and expounded on by Socrates who taught that 'the unexamined life is not worth living'. Will your future employer agree with Socrates on this? I should think that's very likely, so the aspect of self-knowledge is not something that can be underestimated.

In this chapter we will dive deep into the topic of self-awareness in a very practical way. We will give you tips on identifying and deploying your strengths and compare the merits of two key organisational words: passion and professionalism. Whilst the latter word has largely fallen out of use, the former seems to be ever present in all aspects of modern organisational life. We'll investigate which one you should permit to define your approach to work. But before we go there let's just briefly address a very topical subject that currently receives a great deal of media coverage.

The non-stop STEM chatter

On the one hand we hear a great deal these days about teaching kids coding and why particularly girls should study STEM topics and how getting the right degree in something 'practical' is so important. On the other hand, we are, conversely, constantly reminded about Bill Gates and the Google guys and God knows which other tech leaders dropping out of college early and going on to do great things in their garages. The ideal formula for success appears to be to start a technical degree course and then drop out before you graduate.

We must rightfully acknowledge the traditional lack of opportunity particularly for girls in the area of technology and it's completely right that it's being addressed. However, I often meet younger people who feel that perhaps the discipline that attracts them will be regarded as less relevant or important. So here I want to draw your attention to the dangers of simply jumping on the tech study bandwagon at the expense of your personal inclinations and desires. Tech sounds great. It's growing exponentially and provides well-paid jobs in an expanding marketplace. Well maybe that's true as a general statement but it may not be true for you, and that's what really counts. Your competencies, concerns, values and ambitions for your life may not fit into this media-fed hysteria, and you would not be alone. So please don't fall for the hype or be discouraged by the non-stop coding and STEM chatter.

Many very successful people have studied for degrees that would have been regarded by the popular press and many recruiters as less than practical and applicable. For instance, Carl Icahn, the American billionaire investor, graduated from Princeton with a thesis in philosophy entitled *The Problems of Formulating an Adequate Explication of the Empiricist Criterion of Meaning*. George Soros, the activist and philanthropist, and yes also a billionaire, chose philosophy as his topic at college. Out of the last eight British prime ministers three of them, including David Cameron, studied Politics, Philosophy and Economics, as indeed did a host of their political colleagues both in the UK and beyond. Steve Jobs found that his study of calligraphy, and not engineering, was the most important and applicable education he had as he built the Apple empire.

Who says that finding the right word at the right time is less important than writing a line of code? Who says that qualifications in literature, psychology, communication, art or poetry are somehow inferior to those of a technical nature?

Don't be concerned about what topic you studied. It's yours, own it, love it and be proud of it and don't listen to the naysayers. If you are studying robotics or artificial intelligence or engineering, then wonderful; if you are deep into Shakespeare or Goethe or history of art then please carry on. The only demand is that you do your absolute best. Don't forget the technical wizards will meet the design and communication geniuses at work one day and they will quickly find out that neither could have achieved anything worthwhile without the other.

The world's greatest teacher in 2018 was called Andria Zafirakou and she is not teaching kids about technology or even mathematics. She teaches an appreciation for and an understanding of art and textiles to children in London and they love her for it. Education is about learning to think, training is about learning to do; there will be plenty of time for that later.

Do all employers want the same thing?

Some positions that you may be applying for will require very specific knowledge and experience. If you want to pursue a career in, for example, civil engineering, then it's probably a good idea to have pursued a degree course in that subject. We won't explore these specifics here, rather we will focus on what organisations may require in the general sense of hiring people who are subject matter experts but will also fit into the structure and culture of the organisation. Most selection processes will dedicate some time to exploring your specific functional expertise, and increasingly today even more time finding out what kind of a person you are. We will focus mainly on the latter.

A trawl of company websites, recruitment postings and so on can give us a good idea of what kind of personal attributes companies are seeking. YouTube is a veritable goldmine of information on this topic. The former head of HR at Google talks of "hiring for capability and learning ability before expertise" and focusing on hiring "smart, curious people rather that those who are deeply expert in one area." The focus has switched strongly from simply your area of expertise towards your attitude to learning and indeed life. Like Google most companies now want rounded individuals with broad potential to learn and relearn rather than the traditional narrowly focused expert. The days of going to an interview where you can talk non-stop about your brilliant degree and your skills in technology or marketing or whatever have ended. Now they want to know who you are and what you stand for. For you to pass that test you had better have a good answer.

Checking your head and your heart

We started this chapter with a focus on the idea of 'self' and the notion that it's somehow ephemeral, abstract and difficult to pin down. It tends to be particularly so in a world where we are bombarded with images and narratives of how we should look and be. In fact, the more the world tries to define success and happiness for us the more urgent the need is to define our own.

This is a journey that has two aspects to it. Firstly, it's about your willingness to reflect consciously, engage with your thoughts, actions, needs and ambitions, and secondly, your reactions to whatever the world may throw at you. If you are not prepared to look in the mirror voluntarily, then at some point in your life the world will, in one way or another, reflect how it experiences you. Anne Enright, the Irish novelist, sums this up in the phrase "people don't change, they are merely revealed." There is nothing surer than if you don't make the effort then the world someday may reveal a version of you that you may find surprising.

Self-awareness

In corporate speak, all of this falls under the headline of self-awareness. This is the centre of gravity that will be the basis of your development as a person, an employee, a manager and a future leader. That translates into understanding not just your impact on other people but your willingness and ability to learn, grow and change as an individual and as an employee. Let's just try and break that down a little bit more to two basic goals:

1. Becoming self-aware concerning your values, motivations, prevailing attitudes and your impact on others.

2. Finding out what you are good at. Focusing on that will enable you to participate in the world of work and earn a living, do great things, be a leader or whatever your heart's desire may be.

This will involve experiencing a range of things that will confirm or even blow away some long-held beliefs of self. The two above goals are, of course, deeply connected and they will draw on and build on each other as you gain more experience of life and life at work.

How would you know that you were self-aware or, conversely, possessed? Little self-awareness? How might this be expressed in behavioural terms? You would value understanding the impact you make on others and the ensuing benefits of monitoring and improving on that impact, it's important to you. Your interactions would be underpinned by behaviours consistent with the values you hold. You know what you are good at and what you will never be great at and you have accepted that you have both your strengths and weaknesses.

Those who lack self-awareness tend to be less bound to a solid sense of self and the choices they make may be more opportunistic. As a result, they often come across as grasping, arrogant or aloof.

Two perspectives to self-awareness

The layman's understanding of self-awareness tends to be very much built around the notion of introspection. If not head in hands negativity, then deep thought and self-examination. The work of Tasha Eurich shows us that this is of course a necessary but insufficient approach and that self-awareness can ideally be divided into two distinct areas.

The first of these is *internal self-awareness*, representing the clarity with which we see ourselves and our impact on others. The study found that it is associated with many positive aspects such as job and relationship satisfaction, personal and social control, and is negatively related to anxiety, stress and depression.

The second, *external self-awareness*, was described as understanding of how other people view us in terms of those same factors listed above. The research showed that people who know how others see them are more skilled at showing empathy and understanding the point of view of others. For leaders who see themselves as their employees do, their employees tend to have a better relationship with them, feel more satisfied with them, and see them as being more effective in general.

One might expect that being high on *internal self-awareness* would automatically lead to being high on the other. In contrast to what one might expect, the research showed virtually no relationship between them. As a result, four self-awareness archetypes were identified, making it relatively easy for all of us to find our current default approaches as we strive to become more self-aware.

The Four Self-Awareness Archetypes

This 2x2 maps internal self-awareness (how well you know yourself) against external self-awareness (how well you understand how others see you).

	Low external self-awareness	High external self-awareness
High internal self-awareness	**INTROSPECTORS** They're clear on who they are but don't challenge their own views or search for blind spots by getting feedback from others. This can harm their relationships and limit their success.	**AWARE** They know who they are, what they want to accomplish, and seek out and value others' opinions. This is where leaders begin to fully realize the true benefits of self-awareness.
Low internal self-awareness	**SEEKERS** They don't yet know who they are, what they stand for, or how their teams see them. As a result, they might feel stuck or frustrated with their performance and relationships.	**PLEASERS** They can be so focused on appearing a certain way to others that they could be overlooking what matters to them. Over time, they tend to make choices that aren't in service of their own success and fulfillment.

SOURCE DR. TASHA EURICH

© HBR.ORG

Clearly the top right quadrant is where we all want to be, being AWARE, i.e. high on both external and internal self-awareness. Try and find yourself in the matrix above. Which description best fits to you? Be honest and if you are not in the AWARE box start to consider how you might get there and of course this book is packed with ideas to help you achieve just that, and this study gives us a great place to start.

A key finding in answering the question 'How do I become more self-aware?' emerged from this work. Introspection for most of us involves asking ourselves why. Why did I not get my point of view across? Why did I react so negatively? Why did I not see that opportunity?

Moving from the why to the what

Sitting and ruminating on the 'why' often leads to 'unproductive and negative thoughts'. Instead of engaging in the self-torture around the word 'why' the researchers recommend using a different word. When they looked at the introspection strategies of highly self-aware people they found that these people preferred to ask themselves *what* instead of *why* thus identifying *situations that provoked poor performance* rather than the almost unanswerable 'why'. The 'what' question offers practical and impersonal solutions and leads logically to the question 'What can I now do about it?' This is a major finding that can help us break out of the self-incriminating, unanswerable, interminable cycle of painful self-blame.

Is there anything that I'm going to be good at?

You will be great at doing certain tasks and in certain situations and not so good at others. It's a fact of life. Just because you are not great at some stuff does not mean it's a weakness. I know someone who is not very good at reading spreadsheets, but she never let it become a weakness because her choice of occupation does not involve spreadsheets, and if it occasionally does, she knows someone she can send it to. She prefers to call it a non-strength. It may seem trivial, but it reveals an understanding, an acceptance and a coping strategy.

Organisations still love to use the word weakness. Being asked to explain some of your weaknesses is a standard question at most interviews. Liz Ryan thinks that the 'So what's your greatest weakness?' question is akin to asking 'So do you watch much porn?'. She sees it as a presumptuous power play on behalf of the interviewer. In any case what use is the question? If you are applying to be a software engineer you are hardly going to answer 'Well, I was always very bad at maths.' You will probably waffle on about meaningless nonsense just to keep the interviewer happy, and no one gets anything out of the question.

Liz gives a great example of an answer to the weakness question incorporating several parts. "I used to obsess about my deficiencies when I was younger… then I realised that I need to focus on what I was good at… and the stuff I really want to be doing… so these days I don't focus on weaknesses that need correcting… instead I ask myself 'What does the universe want me to do?'." Of course, it sounds a bit bull-shitty, but it was a bullshit question in the first place.

This shows you have thought about the topic, have defined a way forward and 'got over' the endless rumination so many people engage in regarding their 'weaknesses'. That alone is a major achievement. Remember there is a difference between having a weakness and doing stuff you simply don't enjoy doing. You may be a world champion at Excel but after the 27th person has come to your desk looking for help your expertise may take on the attributes of a weakness, as it may interfere with your own work and your mood may not be that welcoming.

Don't resist the flow – where do your strengths want to take you?

The entire area of strengths and talents can be a confusing one with the words like strengths and talents and skills often being interchanged and being poorly understood. Probably the best definition of these words and how they connect available today comes from Clifton Strengths in the Gallup organisation.

"A strength is the ability to consistently provide near-perfect performance in a specific activity. Talents are naturally recurring patterns of thought, feeling, or behaviour that can be productively applied. Talents, knowledge and skills along with the time spent (i.e. investment) practising, developing your skills, and building your knowledge base combine to create your strengths."

It's very nicely summarised in this formula:

$$(Talent + Knowledge + Skills) \times Investment$$

This helps demystify and operationalise the continuum from innate talent to job success. Step one would be to find your talent(s). It can be tricky and often is only revealed by trying out stuff. The thing is you will know when you find it. That's a given. Clifton Strengths summarises the combination of talent, knowledge, skills and investment as follows: "As a salesperson, you can learn your products' features (knowledge), you can be trained to ask the right open-ended questions (skill), and you can practise making a sale (investment). However, the innate tendency to push a customer to commit at exactly the right moment, in exactly the right way, must be naturally occurring and cannot be learned."

This tells us that once we discover our natural talents a whole world of improvement possibilities is available to us. We can build our knowledge and hone our skills through investing in this thing we have been gifted. This is where *investment in strengths* can convert them into something akin to superpowers, i.e. a personal career differentiator that can ensure that you will shine. More on that later, but just don't settle for being mediocre with your gifts.

A nice way of identifying your strengths is to apply the following simple formula to the various tasks that you do (and situations you experience):

$$S = P - E \quad \text{Strength} = \text{Performance} - \text{Effort}$$

TASK	PERFORMANCE	EFFORT	STRENGTH
A	9	1	👍
B	3	7	✗

For example, let's say that you self-evaluate your performance on task A with the highest score being 10 and the lowest 1. You score 9, a very high score that informs us that you are excellent at task A. You then consider how much effort you need to put in to achieve that score, and with the ranking being the same as for the evaluation you conclude that you can perform brilliantly on that task and expend very little effort in doing so. You have identified a key strength. Checking task B you may reach a different conclusion.

Strengths should be grouped as portfolios and never forget that one great strength is never enough. If you want to be a professional basketball player being tall would be a great personal asset to bring to the game. Are the very tallest players always the most successful? No, they are not and the received wisdom on this topic is that after 1.9m height adds little extra to performance. Other strengths come into play to complement and build on 'being tall' as a core strength. Irrespective of height, aggression, motor skills, hand-eye coordination and team ability, for example, come together to bring success on the court. Height alone is not enough.

So do always try to be careful regarding the extent to which you try to exploit your key strengths. The fastest way to turn a strength into a weakness is to overuse it. It's like singing the same song every day, those around you will get sick of it and your voice won't develop.

It's important to remember that not all strengths are equal. You may be brilliantly analytical, focused and precise – wonderful strengths indeed – but without complementary strengths, say in communication and influence, they may never be exercised at the highest level. Communication tends to be the key differentiator that brings other strengths to life. Communication is of course a very general and wide-ranging talent but it does lie at the heart of activating your strengths. There are at least a thousand ways to be a great communicator so please consider what yours might be.

However, not being talented in a certain area does not mean that you can't improve in that area. You may never be a world champion at it, but you can get yourself to a level of competency that will help lift your core strengths to a higher level. So, you have your portfolio of strengths and your next move is to find out just where and on what you want to focus them. The alignment of strengths and their focus on enjoyable, motivational and profitable work is the Nirvana that so many people seek. Do this and you are in the territory where superpowers can emerge.

Your job description is not set in concrete

Many people tell me that they can't find a job that suits their strengths. That's probably for the very good reason that it doesn't exist. It's not about finding a job that suits your strengths that's important, it's about shaping the position you currently occupy to suit your strengths.

Neil McGregor, the author and art historian, went for an interview for the directorship of the British Museum in 2002. The museum was not in a good state being heavily in debt and suffering from dropping visitor numbers. This situation influenced the selection criteria for the position with the Trustees focusing on candidates who could effect a financial and administrative turnaround. McGregor's reputation was that of a 'scholar rather than a manager'. At his interview McGregor did not pretend he was a great administrator. Instead, 'he convinced the museum's Trustees to let him shape the job to suit his strengths' and delegate the administrative part to others on the team. He went on to be one of the most successful directors in the history of the museum.

The key learning here is firstly to be creative and flexible about your strengths based on the opportunity before you, and secondly to see your role in the context of the various tasks and indeed of the entire team.

Passion and professionalism

The word passion is thrown about organisational life as if having lots of it will make you the most wonderful colleague and most valued employee on the planet. I sincerely hope that it's just a passing fashion, because even if you are expressing passion about whatever it is you are doing, it most certainly doesn't mean that you are any good at it.

A friend of mine, who is an IT manager by way of occupation, is a motorcycle enthusiast. He owns several and a good deal of his free time is spent riding and upgrading his bikes. You might say in modern corporate parlance that he is passionate about motorbikes. I asked him once if he would like to work for a motorcycle company. I was somewhat surprised when he answered, "No way." He went on to explain that his enthusiasm for motorbikes overlaps with his interest in being outdoors and travel, his natural ability in working with tools, and the sense of camaraderie he finds hanging out with fellow enthusiasts. He loves his professional position in IT and sees it being balanced by his motorcycle enthusiasm, which permits him to express himself in a more practical and very different way. Mixing the two he finds deeply unattractive. "I'm a professional IT guy and an enthusiastic biker and that's the way I want to keep it," he concluded.

Lucy Kellaway, the *Financial Times* journalist, relates a story of addressing a group of tax accountants and asking them if they were passionate about their work. Most raised their hands to say they were. But after she told them she herself really did not feel much passion for her job, "I'm lucky to have it and it suits me," and when she pointed out that passion properly refers to "strong sexual attraction or to the suffering of Jesus Christ in the lead up to his crucifixion," the passionate numbers in the group declined to almost zero when asked a second time.

We hear a lot about finding your passion and expressing it at work. Lots of companies apparently want you to do this. We are most familiar with the expression of passion in the artistic sense. Singers and musicians had better at some point express passion onstage or we simply don't buy their art. Looking heavenwards and closing the eyes is a common way they express their passion. You may not want to try this sitting before your screen in an open plan office on a wet Tuesday afternoon.

Andre Agassi, who won eight major tennis titles and was at one point number one in the world, may have looked passionate as he slogged away on tennis courts and living, at least what appeared to be, the dream of so many.

Imagine being a sports superstar earning truckloads of cash, travelling the world and being revered by legions of fans. Who could have guessed that beneath the passionate veneer lay a deep level of discontent and unhappiness with his profession and lifestyle? Passion is of course eminently easy to fake. Stay late, look serious, cry now and again as your passion overwhelms you. Eat, sleep and dream about your job and you will be crowned the passion queen of the office. Good luck with that.

When Lucy Kellaway looked up passion as a job requirement in recruitment advertisements on Glassdoor.com she found 34,000 hits. When she entered conscientiousness she got only 1,345. Fox News in the US recently advertised for a writer with 'a passion for accuracy' of all things. That's how a fashionable word can go viral.

Would you rather be arrested by a passionate or professional police officer?

Or indeed would you rather share an office with a passionate person or a conscientious one? Of course, the real problem here is the choice of the word. How at an interview could the interviewer test for passion? Would an answer that you will work night and day be enough? Would tears at the very mention of your professional choice of job get you in the door? If I see a general understanding of passion at work today then it tends to be the teary and 'I'll do long hours to prove it' understanding that prevails. So be careful when passion comes up at interviews and discussions at work as you may be setting up some false expectations. My biker friend mentioned the word professionalism which was how he described himself at work.

Professional is a word that has somehow slipped between the cracks of modern organisational speak. It conjures up a picture of a person who is qualified, experienced and knowledgeable in their area of expertise. Someone whose judgment you can trust and someone who represents a body of knowledge and is qualified to speak on it. Professionalism also speaks to pride and even appearance. We have all heard the maxim 'she looked and sounded really professional'.

Passion and professionalism are not mutually exclusive, some people exhibit both; however, leaders and organisations will generally place a premium on one or the other through the language they use. The New York Police Department are very clear about what kind of people they want to attract. Check out what is written on the side of their vehicles.

Credit JaysonPhotography

If we contrast the words professional and passionate, we can certainly see some overlaps in terms of commitment and drive. However, underlying the word passion is the assumption that 'passionate' people are somehow gaining personal meaning from the outcome of their work. The word professional conveys a more neutral impression – professional distance – of someone focusing on doing things properly and well, whatever the final product of the work may be.

Bill Wiersma in his book *The Power of Professionalism* writes of his interviews with employees at a particularly successful company, which was well known for their ability to engage their employees, despite producing a product that would probably not inspire passion in many people. Sally Helgeson summarised his findings nicely, writing that 'meaning was not vested in the product or outcome, rather in how the daily experience of doing your work helps you develop as a human being'. She was referring to a professional, respectful atmosphere which focused on the execution of the strategy and associated tasks. Meaning was embedded in the quality of the human interaction and subsequent growth and development of all. It's a nice analysis which reminds us that professionalism is not devoid of personal satisfaction and, dare we say, meaning, quite the contrary.

Check out the language of any company you may be considering joining and note the balance they show between being passionate and being professional and then conclude where you would feel you would fit in best. Like my biker friend you can be enthusiastic about whatever you want outside of work and lead a professional career that's balanced and complemented by these other pursuits that you enjoy.

Work, Learn, Play, Move – Tips for the Newbie You

1. Go to your boss before she comes to you

Never wait for her to say, "I want to see you in my office." Initiating check-ins with your direct boss clearly demonstrates that you are an independent self-starter. The check-ins can be focused on getting advice or coaching or simply showing curiosity about the strategy and how you may be helpful. Show this behaviour and you begin to build trust. As a result, your boss will be more easily persuaded when you want to make alterations to your role or have suggestions for improvements.

2. Get your strengths up and running

Take your job and look at it through the filter of your strengths. Then slowly begin to shape your tasks, communication and collaboration requirements to play to your strengths. Maybe you can do trade-offs with fellow team members as a way of moving on aspects that really don't work well for you. Build towards your Superpower status by testing yourself in different situations and tasks. You'll know when you find it.

3. Don't complain

Blowing off steam with people at work who understand where you are coming from is a big temptation. Forget it as there is no upside to it. Take your frustrations to the gym or running track and try to have real solid problem-solving conversations with someone close to you outside of work.

4. Take charge of your time

People often sit around the office waiting for the boss to leave. They don't want to be seen leaving before him. Getting up and saying 'See you tomorrow' to everyone at the normal finishing time is a public statement of your independence. If you can show that you are the boss of your own calendar and time, then you have gone a long way to empowering yourself. Have a plan, have a schedule, have a private life and you will find that, after some time, people will start to adapt to your schedule, but only if you really mean it and show consistency.

5. Clarify your role and deliverables

You have the right to know what your role entails. You have a right to know your goals and objectives and how your success will be measured. If you don't get them in writing, then write them up yourself and go through them with your boss. Have boundaries regarding 'shared team goals' and make sure those you work closely with are aware of them.

6. Be in learning mode

Work is a much richer learning environment than college. If the actual tasks you are allocated are not as stimulating as you would like, then set yourself a learning agenda. Companies are full of learning and development opportunities and smart people. Get to know both and expand your learning opportunities.

7. Have lots going on in your life

I have heard the time when you are not at work referred to by some commentators as 'discretionary time'. What a weird statement. Like it was anyone's business. It's no one's business except yours. Use your time as you wish. A great life outside of work will make a great workplace life even better and will offer relief from a poor workplace experience. Don't let work become the be all and end all of who you are. It's not.

8. Move on

Don't hang around too long, not even if you have the greatest boss in the universe. People all too often let their boss morph into being their mentor, shoulder to cry on and general guarantor of their career and life security. Don't do this. If you are young enough to try different stuff, then say thanks and leave on great terms and always stay in touch.

Summary

Work will challenge you in unexpected ways. All the hard work you put in at college or indeed on the sports field may not be regarded in the way you might think it should be. It's best to think about these qualifications as a ticket to the game rather than any form of entitlement. Examine your own life and your motivations, values and ambitions because if you don't do this privately, work may do it to you publicly. Beware of organisational fads like, for instance, passion and the like, and really get to know your strengths. Stay in learning mode and remember you are now working for money. Always respect that contract.

Oscar Wilde said, "Be yourself; everyone else is already taken."

Be that person online, offline, at home, with your friends, at your interview and at work.

- Study what you want to study and work at the job you want to work at and don't feel you have to follow any trend or fashion. These tend to change rapidly in any case, and you will continue to be you.

- Gaining self-awareness is a prerequisite for real and authentic advancement both personally and professionally. It won't happen by magic and requires effort, focus and practice.

- How you see yourself and seek to improve yourself should be informed by your own questions starting with 'what?'. Don't torture yourself with the constant 'why' question.

- What are your natural talents? Which do you want to practise until they become world-class strengths that energise you and excite others? Be aware of what you are not good at and work with others to complete the team strengths jigsaw.

- Will you talk passionately and work professionally? Be aware of the difference and the expectations of the organisation and those with whom you work most closely.

CHAPTER TWO

The Boss Would Like A Word

"I want them to fear how much they love me!"

The Office (US version)

The film *The Cloverfield Paradox* takes place mostly in a space station. After a series of catastrophes that the extremely diligent international crew could not control, one of them in frustration cries out, "I am a physicist" to which the captain of the station replies, "Yeah, and now you work for money." When you start working for money, unless you are a startup entrepreneur working for yourself or have inherited wealth, everything changes. Your Master's degree counts in getting you to that point and hopefully will be helpful to you in doing a great job, but as Gary Vaynerchuk famously wrote: 'Nobody gives a f**k that you were captain of the lacrosse team' and that is no exaggeration; and nobody at work really gives a f**k about your Master's or even your PhD.

I have, more than once, met very highly qualified people lost inside an organisation because they could not comprehend that their brilliant academic careers did not speak for themselves.

Money talks

Working for money practically guarantees that you will have a boss. You may even have two at once or maybe two or three different ones in your first year. It's a vital relationship and the objective of this chapter is to enlighten you regarding this relationship and how to get the most from it. You can learn a great deal from bosses whom you admire and indeed from those who you feel could do better. Remember, despite everything you come with a sign hanging around your neck that reads 'untested' or 'has potential' and getting paid to work should generate a sense of urgency in you, a focus on reality and a mentality that respects the contract that you have entered. So, don't ever fall back on the 'I am a physicist' argument with your boss or, even more importantly, with yourself.

In this chapter we will build your understanding of the challenges bosses face, as it's important that you gain an understanding of the context your boss works in. We will then help you better understand just how to evaluate what kind of person you are reporting to through a variety of lenses. You will get a framework to help you gauge his level of trustworthiness. We relate standard statements bosses make and break then down to their real meanings.

We then look at a couple of key characteristics of great bosses and investigate some of the fatal flaws you will need to be aware of.

From LinkedIn to the water cooler

There are many sources where you can begin to get some impressions of what kind of a person your boss is. How he portrays himself on LinkedIn can be revealing. Check out his experience and interests and particularly how he describes his current position. How he depicts this will tell you a lot about him. Does he come across as modest and authentic or self-important and delusional? Has he had six jobs in the last three years or has he progressed along a more stable career path? LinkedIn, Twitter and other online platforms can be extremely helpful in helping you form at least an initial picture of the person to whom you will be reporting. Does he have recommendations from team members and colleagues, or has he recommended others? In addition, Glassdoor.com can help you gain an impression of the company and context you both will be working in. Your colleagues will also be a source of information about him.

Bosses and their perceived capabilities or lack thereof are a favourite topic of discussion amongst those whom they manage. In most organisations, the 'what I think of the boss' conversations tend to happen at a certain location and at specific times pretty much every day. The location is the water cooler or coffee machine and the rough times are at about 11am and 3pm. A couple of things for you to remember here. Firstly, these water cooler meetings rarely tend to focus on the positive attributes of the boss, and it can be all too easy to get sucked into a bitching session.

The people who dominate these discussions tend to be those who have become disengaged for one reason or another and are trying to win followers over to their point of view. If you find that to be the case, then take your drink and get out of there. Secondly, try to understand that being a leader at any level in business is a non-trivial job and one that's often underestimated by the people being led. Please don't be too quick to condemn, criticise or categorise your manager, that would be both unfair and a mistake.

Middle seat management

When you start in an organisation you will most likely be reporting to what's commonly termed a middle manager. It's the least comfortable position in the organisation and it's comparable to sitting in the middle seat on an aeroplane. The person in the window seat can at least see the big picture outside the window and the person in the aisle seat can come and go and interact with others as he wishes. If the people on either side are bigger, then the person in the middle may get squashed. Most inconveniently, the window and aisle seat fellow travellers may strike up a conversation in which the person in the middle is not invited to participate. Worst of all, if the window seat occupant has a weak bladder then life can be hell. It's a very vulnerable position to be in.

It can be intimidating for your boss to be caught between two big personalities. Their elbows can impinge on his space in a tussle for the armrest, they may have large amounts of carry-on baggage all over the floor. If his superior in the window seat is constantly disturbing him and his team members it can be a very tricky position indeed. For your part try to avoid striking up work-related conversations with your boss's superior that exclude him. It's a cardinal sin.

Keep in mind that a certain power is bestowed on a person when they take charge and people respond in different ways. Some get too close to those they are managing and focus on being part of the group. They may feel insecure with power or indeed may not want it at all. These people may want to be 'friends' with everyone, and the group may lack direction as they try to maintain harmony at all costs.

Others may see power 'as having power over others'. They may assume that now they are the chosen one, they need to act accordingly and become bossy in the worst sense of the word. They may try to manage from a distance and focus only on tasks and results and be very selective about who their 'friends' are. This style can of course alienate members of the group and cause friction and conflict. There is a myriad of responses and styles that managers may demonstrate with the demands of the organisation and especially their direct boss providing the impetus. The middle seat syndrome strikes again.

Are bosses born or made?

People become bosses for all kinds of reasons. Recruiters both internal and external would have us believe that their systems of matching positions to applicants run with a smooth and scientific certainty, and of course there are brilliant systems and dedicated people who do this every day. However, when you get inside an organisation you will find a fair few people who did not emerge from the 'official' evaluation process. Many were simply in the right place at the right time or indeed knew the right person.

Someone once told me an anecdote about a person who happened to walk by an office while speaking Spanish to a colleague. A senior person seated in the office jumped out of his seat, invited him in and after ten minutes offered him a job where competence in Spanish was a key element. Others report being told that they were 'the natural choice' (usually when no one else was willing), and one I remember was informed that he had better say yes because "you won't be asked again." Qualifications, training and suitability counted for little here and never forget that the everyday pressures and demands of organisational life can throw up wonderful opportunities if you are ready to take them.

However, most people who rise to a supervisory position do so because of great performance in their functional job. A great engineer may be promoted to become a manager based on his ability to deliver great engineering solutions. Or a high-performing accountant may be asked to become manager of the accounts department based on his track record as an accountant. The challenge here is that leading engineers or accountants is vastly different from being one. One HR leader told me that his company specialised in turning great engineers into terrible managers. The greatest engineer and the most brilliant accountant soon discover that the skills that got them recognised as candidates for management will not help them when they become a manager.

The chances are that your boss will have been pretty good at whatever his functional expertise was and will have been promoted on that basis. But on becoming the boss he will have inherited a multiplicity of jobs that have zero to do with his functional expertise and for which his education probably did not prepare him. The engineer or accountant will have spent from three to six years at college learning their craft. Suddenly they land in a position where the main subject matter of their new job, i.e. leading other people towards a common goal, barely merited a mention throughout their professional training. If you have a discussion with HR in most organisations about this, they wiggle a bit and say something like, "Yeah, but he is great with people too!" Maybe, but I have never heard of someone who was 'really good with people' but mediocre at his functional tasks being promoted to a position where being 'good with people' was the main criterion for the promotion.

In the business or on the business?

The transition from functional expert to leading people can be a painful and for some an unachievable transition. Michael Gerber calls this a change from 'working *in* the business to working *on* the business'. If your boss is working *on* the business then he will be busy creating the context, organisation and systems that will facilitate your success. These would involve motivating, planning, coaching, dealing with conflicts and team issues and generally operating from a long-term strategic perspective. If he has not made the transition and stays working *in* the business and working at the level of the daily operations, then life may not be too pleasant for you. Chances are that he will be checking on the operational details of your work and probably telling you how to do it better instead of developing your skills and those of the team around you. This person is drawn back to the skills where he excels and feels comfortable exercising instead of learning the leadership skills he needs to work *on* the business. This is not an uncommon occurrence.

Education and experience

Some bosses you will encounter will have gone to elite universities, some will have a secondary school diploma. One of the finest I ever worked with left school at 16 and started driving a truck. He was modest, warm, practical, demanding, consistent, proactive and fun. He was loved by those who reported to him. Another I worked with had a PhD in physics and displayed almost the same qualities with the same positive impact on his people.

Education is a poor predictor of the traits I outlined above. Some may have an MBA which will have some leadership modules as part of the course. Others may have attended an in-company workshop on leading and managing, and others may have had little or no preparation at all for the challenge of leading other people. It's not always competence, courage and ambition that got them into the middle seat. Sometimes, as we have discussed, it may have simply been circumstance. Some never really wanted it in the first place but went with the flow, got used to the rewards and decided to hang on. Others can get intoxicated by the power. Organisational life can be very challenging for the occupants of the middle seat.

Changing organisational structures may eventually make the middle seat redundant, but somehow I doubt it. And very flat organisations present a whole new set of challenges in any case. More on that in other chapters. Most managers are hard-working decent men and women who care deeply about those whom they manage. Some will be affected by the stresses and strains of managing in poorly designed organisations and constant change. Some should never have been promoted in the first place and may be more in need of your support and sympathy than your criticism and judgment. Be a decent and respectful fellow traveller as you occupy your aisle seat. Someday the middle seat or even the window seat may be yours.

How do you know if you can trust your boss?

Trust is a very popular word when teams gather and start discussing their team effectiveness. 'We need more trust…' is the platitude to end all platitudes. It is also rather meaningless and offers us no clue as to how we may proceed either as a group or as an individual in understanding just how we move beyond our gut feeling about others in establishing trusting relationships. Professor Onora O'Neill, the philosopher, has provided a very useful breakdown of the notion of trust that gives us a better handle on understanding this overused word. She vehemently opposes the oft heard mantra 'we need more trust'. Instead she calls for more trust in the trustworthy and less trust in the untrustworthy. For example, placing trust in an untrustworthy character like Bernie Madoff the American financier who, some years back, cheated his clients out of lots of money and is now in prison, was a big mistake made by many people.

But how would you evaluate the trustworthiness of another person including your boss? It's not a simple thing to do accurately as the unfortunate investors in Madoff's company discovered. A sensible question to ask when a person's trustworthiness is being considered is 'Trust him to do what?'. O'Neill gives the example of trusting a child's mathematics teacher to teach the kids maths but perhaps not trusting that same person to drive the school bus. This is a much fairer way to think about the idea of trust and helps demystify the word.

She then breaks it down further and gives us an operational framework for considering the trustworthiness of bosses and indeed anyone else. This consists of three words:

Competence: This takes us back to the 'trust him to do what?' level of specificity. Can the person perform the tasks inherent to their position at a consistently high level? Your leader will have many tasks, and for you it would be best to simply consider his competence in the general sense of his ability to lead and coach the team and not trying to solve all the problems himself.

Honesty: Is the person going to lie, withhold information, do secret deals with some team members? Is he honest with colleagues and customers? Does he have a set of values that are solid? Does he deal with his boss in a straightforward way, or does he obfuscate and withhold information?

Reliability: To be reliable is simply to deliver whatever it is you promised at the right quality on time. 'You can count on Linda, she always delivers' or 'You need to keep an eye on Jack and ensure he gets it in on time.' Some people develop reputations for reliability and others less so. I'm pretty sure we have all worked with competent and honest bosses but with different levels of reliability. Reliability regarding time and quality is harder than it ever has been in this world of complexity and change. So be somewhat forgiving of this measure, less so of lack of competence and never on dishonesty.

Five statements bosses make that you should be wary of

There is an adage that goes 'people don't leave companies they leave bosses'. All the anecdotal evidence and much of the empirical evidence supports this. Your experience of even the greatest company in the world and what it offers will largely be determined by the person you report to. Therefore, we have endeavoured to simplify the process of assessing your superior through the language that he uses and some key attributes and behaviours he may exhibit.

1. My door is always open

This is a common nonsense phrase that managers who are probably not that interested in the welfare of their people often roll out to their subordinates. It's like a get out of jail free card that covers all possibilities and situations. 'Well you know I said my door is always open.' It's basically an abdication of responsibility, a general offer that has no substance except as an arse-covering generality. What it does is place all responsibility on the subordinate to act. It's what I term 'a walk away statement' as the times I have heard it the person talking was usually walking away and looking over their shoulder.

2. You guys need to sort this out

It's weird. People often for no discernible reason simply meet other people to whom they cannot relate and take a dislike to. Everyone thinks they are the exception to this rule. I did. You may have as well. But sooner or later you find out that Mary who sits in the corner by the window simply doesn't like you. It's all a matter of degree of course, and disagreement can be expressed in many ways. Two people may not get along but simply leave it at that and avoid each other in a passive defensive way as much as possible. People may be competing for the boss's attention and that can cause friction.

The resolution of conflict has historically been one of the main and most public tasks of leaders from the village headman to the king. Just check out *Game of Thrones*. Bullying or harassment should never be accepted. If your boss won't act, then go to his boss. A refusal to act on their part can encourage bullying and politics and victimisation. People who steal ideas and take undue credit should be challenged on the spot, again no waiting. Beware, some bosses like to see conflict in the team as it can divert attention from themselves. If that is the case with your boss either escalate according to company policy or find a new boss. You don't need to sort it out, rather you, the other person and your boss do.

3. Everyone listen up, we must stop working in silos

This is a big favourite. You hear senior managers, particularly at all employee meetings, practically begging people to 'break down the silos'. Silo comes from agricultural storage where products are stored alongside but separate from each other in large upright containers – silos. In the case of organisational collaboration silos refer to the tendency that business units and departments have to hoard information and resources, instead of sharing with other parts of the business. One company I know staged a mock funeral with a coffin containing the dreaded 'silo mentality' being buried. This had an enormous effect for about one day and then things went back to their usual state.

However, whilst this phrase has been repeated a gazillion times by managers it's very rare indeed to hear serious solutions being offered. Attention from those in charge to some simple and consistent process management and overall communication would help. This is not an insurmountable problem but hearing this refrain time and again from management without any defined actions can be a depressing experience. You can do your part by deliberately getting to know your upstream/downstream colleagues and their work and inviting them to get to know yours. A good way to accomplish this is to occasionally invite them to your meetings and request an invitation to theirs.

4. Jimmy in accounts receivables is doing an amazing job

Michael Gerber reminds us of the inherent dangers of your boss constantly using your name or those of your colleagues instead of referring to your functions. This may seem rather trivial, but if he consistently says things like "I really don't know what we would do without Dave in procurement," then he is personalising the success he is referring to, i.e. it's due to the person sitting in that chair. That indeed may be the case but it does nothing for the development of the position itself. It tends to load the success on to the efforts of the individual in question. It's a subtle means of exerting pressure on people by publicly elevating them. How will Dave feel when things are not going so well? Will he be listened to if he requests more resources or will he be expected to work 24/7 to save what amounts to his public reputation?

I witnessed such a situation myself. A young manager had performed heroic deeds rescuing a project and made a presentation to colleagues that included what was almost a boast, of late nights, long weekends and neglected family time. He was amazed when his audience regarded his 'success' with icy silence. The boss's job is to optimise the function irrespective of who is responsible and not to fawn over the current occupant in this passive-aggressive way. This happens a lot. Of course, names have been used and success recognised, but try and learn the difference between honest praise and subtle pressure. Accept and enjoy the former, be aware of and don't fall for the latter.

5. Let me tell you what the problem is

This is a key differentiator. If your boss is constantly saying things like "Thanks, but this is how it really works!" or "Don't do it like that, Jack tried that last year and it was a disaster" or "Here's the problem with that!" you really need to understand that you may have chosen an idiot for a boss and consider if you want to stay. The persistent use of these kind of statements leaves you no room for creativity or imagination and imposes a solution to whatever you are working on, on you. They constitute a full stop on discussion and debate.

As the drawing below illustrates, the exclamation marks following these kinds of statements can become a kind of prison locking up your intelligence, ideas and curiosity. You will feel locked in and confined as you try to work within the parameters of these statements. You will quickly find out that this is not a sustainable situation. Don't even think of asking this boss for feedback.

On the other hand, if your boss prods you to think through the challenges you face by asking you questions that expand your thinking about the problem and encourages you to find your own solution, then your boss selection process has been a success. Check out the two reversed question marks below. Yes, it's a heart. You may even fall in love with a boss who honours and respects you by drawing out your smarts, experience and creativity and in doing so sets you free to continuously learn. But let's be fair, sometimes your boss may have to get something done immediately and may impose a solution and that's fine, but only if it's the exception and not the rule. And you are not seeking perfection, you are looking for his default approach i.e. what's his preferred and usual method? My advice: exit fast if his default approach is the mind prison.

Two key attributes you should look for in your boss

Does he have a sense of humour?

Laughter eats ego for lunch (apologies to Peter Drucker) in the sense that true laughter requires a certain letting go. It's an out of control state and must be, if it's real and authentic. Your ego needs to sink into your shoes for it to be so. Your boss may not want his ego anywhere near his shoes. He may regard being out of control for one millisecond as terrifying, as he may believe that being in control is the meaning of being a boss. Laughter is a great equaliser and for him to find the same thing funny as you do would be to bring himself down to your level. This is a shocking thought for some. 'I'm the boss, I'm smarter, have a bigger car, earn more money, went to a top school – how can I be laughing at the same joke as these bozos, this is dangerous?' Having read somewhere that it's important to socialise and to circumvent this situation, you will occasionally see a normally humourless boss attempt to contrive a situation where he can tell some lame joke and maintain control. Few things are more pathetic to witness than the boss trying to balance being light-hearted and maintain his 'I'm in charge' demeanour at the same time.

The real test is his ability to see the funny side of his own shortcomings. If he cannot be to some extent self-deprecating and accepting of his own fallibility, then I would proceed with caution. Humour is part of the human condition. It's an energiser and tension reducer at work and indeed an opportunity to truly share part of yourself with your colleagues.

Does he have a point of view?

The most vital thing that you are looking for in your new boss is a point of view. That means having a core set of perspectives emanating from his position that are clear, consistent and communicated. This point of view will encompass his role, strategy, business, customers and other aspects of the business. It means that he has engaged with his role, thought about different perspectives and will make a stand if necessary. This should not be confused with a fixed and immovable point of view, but a set of beliefs and commitments which he can explain logically and which he clearly believes in.

If he does not possess a point of view, not only does it cause confusion in his team but he leaves himself, and you, open to whatever strategies, solutions and tasks that come down the chain of command to him. It's his job to challenge what arrives on his desk from above, agree what makes sense and agree what does not. Without personal convictions he will have no real way to argue his case and may end up accepting all manner of assignments and projects that could end up landing on your desk. You would expect that such people would not last very long in most organisations, but you may well be surprised. Life can be stressful and unpredictable under such a leader. My advice: get out fast.

Does your boss suffer from either of these conditions?

The Dunning-Kruger Syndrome

Over two centuries ago Voltaire said, "To be certain about something, one must know either everything or nothing about it." At least the second part of his statement has been proven valid by the research into the Dunning-Kruger syndrome. We have all met people who simply cannot estimate just how little they know about a topic with any degree of accuracy. They are not stupid in the general sense, they simply do not possess the ability to understand just how incompetent they may be at something. However, they behave as if they were world experts on the topic and exude confidence and swagger in their erroneous belief.

This is where it can be dangerous in a manager. When this false confidence is combined with the role authority that being a manager bestows, then any debate about the merits of any idea or concept in the team can be quickly neutralised by the person who possesses such certainty. A manager with the Dunning-Kruger syndrome will be unlikely to let others persuade him that he may not be 100% right about the topic of the day. Such people tend not to be very self-aware and probably won't ask for help and will come across as uninterested in others' perspectives. Check the chart below: if your boss is low on experience / competence, then you may be in for a rough ride. Head for the exit would be my advice. I really don't see people who are like this changing.

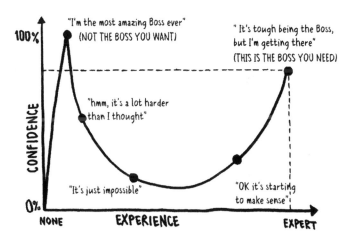

The Imposter Syndrome

This is pretty much the exact opposite of the Dunning-Kruger. In this case people feel they are out of their depth, really don't deserve the position that they hold and live in perpetual fear of being 'found out'. I once heard a senior vice president in a large global organisation inform a room full of colleagues that in his 25 years at the firm, he came to work each day fearing that he would get fired for incompetence. Despite being an accomplished leader who had won the respect of his peers, he had never shaken off this sense of dread and not being good enough. He feared that it all could end at any moment. We can all on occasions feel inadequate, but this condition describes people for whom these feelings are a constant companion.

It's a matter of degree of course, but very strong feelings of inadequacy can be crippling. Most people who make it to a management position in a company won't, hopefully, be so badly affected. However, if your boss does suffer to some extent from the imposter syndrome, then he may well be in some famous company. Sheryl Sandberg, the COO of Facebook, reports such feelings as do the actors Tom Hanks and Emma Watson and, indeed, a host of other high achievers. The negative side of this may be fatigue, self-criticism and occasionally an inability to enjoy accomplishments and success. These people tend to be a bit fragile but endearing, modest and striving. All in all, they tend to make decent bosses as they are usually conscientious and fair. Make sure you are equally conscientious and fair in your dealings with them.

Summary

Like all 'firsts', you will remember your first boss, and you will use that experience as the template for evaluating future bosses and managing upwards as your working life goes forwards. Your antennae as you begin in your first job will be as sharp as they ever will be. You will show up on day one with bigger ears, faster hands and a positive mentality. Seize the opportunity; work, learn, take notes, ask questions, experiment a little and stay conscious and mindful as you begin to figure out managing the critical relationship between yourself and your boss. Remember that it's a two-way street and your ability to manage your relationship with your boss well will be an ability that will serve you well for your entire career.

- Here we have given you a timely reminder that when you work for money someone will be supervising that work and that relationship is the most important one you have inside the organisation.

- It's very likely that your boss sits in the middle of the organisation with the dual pressures from above and below squeezing his time, effectiveness, and in many cases sanity.

- All kinds of people become bosses. Some may be highly educated, some less so. This tells us little about their effectiveness. Many will have risen through the ranks by sheer hard work. Others may have been in the right place at the right time.

- Observe how your boss addresses different topics. Does he provide a good balance between managing his people and getting results?

- Does he provide clarity around goals, objectives and future direction? Can he communicate and represent this point of view?

- Is he self-deprecating or defensive about his own shortcomings or arrogant and boastful, or is he more self-critical and concerned about his own abilities?

CHAPTER THREE

Culture Is Something That You Feel

"Culture eats strategy for lunch."

Peter Drucker

I sometimes wonder how the word culture was chosen to represent the working environment in organisations. It's a complex, opaque word borrowed from the field of anthropology no less and it's often not well understood in the world of business. In the corporate setting at least, culture has tended to be represented by a set of company values. Usually these values present a pretty big target for anyone who is not a fully-fledged sociopath to hit. Stuff like Integrity, Innovation, Collaboration and Teamwork are hardly difficult to nod your head to. Have a trawl through the websites of companies you are considering approaching and see what you can learn. But don't be too disappointed if you find the same old stuff gets repeated ad nauseam.

Personally, when the discussion of values arises in corporate leadership events I try to ensure that there are no sharp implements in the room, and we are not more than two storeys off the ground. Check the eye rolls and disengagement when the same old set of meaningless jargon is rolled out by the CEO, or whoever, at the annual conference and then put back in their box for another year.

An executive once remarked to me that values that have been publicly espoused by an organisation but not really embraced and operationalised tend to become counterproductive. He said it's like leaving dead fish lying around, 'they tend to smell after a while', meaning that it would have been better not to bother with them at all in the first place. I could not agree more. A very recent survey by Board Agenda together with Mazars and INSEAD reached some startling conclusions about the time dedicated to this issue at board level. 'The agenda time for culture appears to be absent for many, potentially undermining the ability of boards to set a tone from the top.' However, the scariest and most telling outcome was that a majority do not even regard culture as a potential risk factor.

This chapter is going to help you get a feel for organisations you may be considering joining. Your gut feeling really is the way to evaluate culture; the posters, cards and website promises inform you of nothing worthwhile. You will also get some tips to help you distinguish positive cultures from negative and toxic ones. In addition, you will build a better understanding of the vital importance of culture as a hard business priority.

Values in the mail

In January 2013 the former CEO of Barclays Bank, Antony Jenkins, wrote a 'Purpose & Values' letter to the entire organisation. He wrote: 'There is no doubt that 2012 was a difficult year for Barclays and the entire banking sector. Again, financial institutions found themselves too often in the news for the wrong reasons. This damaged trust in banks, which was already at a low ebb, and overshadowed the excellent and valued work you do.' He laid out the values of the bank – Respect, Integrity, Service, Excellence and Stewardship – and he implored his management and employees to live by them.

The central idea was that compensation levels would be aligned with your ability to adhere to the values. He wrote: 'I have no doubt that the overwhelming majority of you will enthusiastically support this move. But there might be some who don't feel they can fully buy into an approach which so squarely links performance to the upholding of our values. My message to those people is simple: Barclays is not the place for you. The rules have changed. You won't feel comfortable at Barclays and, to be frank, we won't feel comfortable with you as colleagues.'

Fair enough you might say; he has laid down the law and you better get with the programme if you want to survive, and what's not to like about the list of values he outlined?

Well, consider for a moment a large financial institution having to inform employees and customers that it values 'integrity'. Surely the most basic aspect of managing people's hard-earned cash is that you will be honest in dealing with it.

Imagine you are pregnant (if you can), and the baby is about to arrive. When you arrive at the maternity ward you see a big sign hanging on the wall that says:

WE LOVE BABIES AND AVOID DROPPING THEM AT ALL TIMES

In this case you might get more than a tad nervous and head for a different hospital. Value statements are meant to offer a sense of trust, security and indeed optimism. So why would anyone feel compelled to let you know that they won't do bad things to you, or in the case of a bank with your money?

On careful reading of the letter you notice that he could not maintain the values argument for very long. After espousing the values approach, one page later he reverts to the good old-fashioned and easily understood: 'The rules have changed.' Basically, he was tacitly admitting that this values stuff is fluffy corporate speak in a place where clarity and consequence were sorely needed.

Why did he even bother with this so-called value statement in the first place? Why use yet another word that people find difficult to understand and articulate? Why not just lay out your five rules for working at the company and then people would get it? If we were to convert the five values above into simple rules, they might read something like this:

1. Respect: *Do not engage in politics, bullying or intimidation.*

2. Integrity: *Do not lie, cheat, scam or steal.*

3. Service: *Remember the money we work with belongs to the people who earned it.*

4. Excellence: *Do not accept less than the highest standards.*

5. Stewardship: *Do not make self-serving short-term decisions.*

Of course, I am being facetious, but you can't deny that when you remove the values fluff it's uncanny how much more impactful the words become. I just wonder what the shareholders and indeed employees would vote for given the chance. Values fluff or clarity?

But let's be clear, values are meant to offer both moral (do the right thing) guidance and drive behavioural and leadership alignment. They should underpin your decisions, and in particular difficult decisions you may have to make alone and quickly. There should be a shared framework that accelerates the workings of an organisation through consistency of thought and action from top to bottom. Without a common commitment to some standard of integrity and behaviour you are dependent on individual responses in what are often very stressful situations. But most importantly, it's the formulation, communication and above all the skill and commitment of the top team in translating them into meaningful actions that really counts.

The multi-billion dollar cultural emissions mess

The emissions scandal at Volkswagen is a perfect example of this simply not functioning. In brief, this involved the deliberate manipulation of test emissions that gave testing authorities the impression that their diesel cars were compliant with the environmental laws governing emissions. This was not a one-off error, rather a long-term, systemic effort to deceive, involving the installation of illegal software to produce false readings. It cost the company tens of billions in revenue and profit, reputations were shredded and at least one manager went to prison in the US. Let's look at their pre-crisis values statement.

'Sustainable, collaborative and responsible thinking underlies everything that we do.' It's not really a bad statement at all. It's appealing in its simplicity and focus and could well form the basis of a great place to work. So, for example, you as a new employee walk into work there on your first day and you have every right to expect a working environment that reflects the above statement. That's the promise they have made to you as an employee. The following extract from Patrick Magee's article in the *Financial Times* clearly shows the gap between values fantasy and daily reality:

"One VW insider says taking the decision-making process away from a small circle of people is 'a real need'. Under former VW chairman Ferdinand Piëch and Mr Winterkorn, he says, 'the top-top management of VW went after every single detail'. Often what happened was that when the key people were not available to look at the details, no decision was taken at all. Everybody was afraid of doing something wrong."

So much for sustainable, collaborative and responsible thinking. Oliver Schmidt, the VW manager who went to prison in the US, claimed in a letter to the judge he felt 'misused' by the company. Surely an understatement. Deceiving employees through values statements in this case ended in the deception of customers, shareholders and the general public and cost the company billions. That's not to mention the environmental damage and, in the case of Mr Schmidt, getting a prison sentence in a foreign country. You should note that the outcomes of managing in such a toxic culture can have the gravest of consequences for the individual. The odour of dead fish permeates all aspects of this case.

But the important part is how companies deal with these setbacks, how they restore the confidence of both employees and consumers in the brand. One senior VW manager was accused of trying to 'use the scandal to accelerate cost-cutting'. Please stay conscious of the fact that cost-cutting usually means the cuts will occur pretty much everywhere except at the top of the organisation. The new CEO Mr Müller employed a 'board member for integrity' which was I guess a good idea. However, the Board Agenda study states that "Appointing a single board member will not work if the other board members do not understand the language and distinctions that seek to address issues." Again, the complexity of the issue leads to knee-jerk solutions. How integrity will be managed he did not say, nor was there any elaboration around getting board members up to speed on the 'language and distinctions'.

In an interview with NPR radio in January 2016 in the US he was asked what his plan was to restore the company after the scandal. This challenge the interviewer presented as 'mountain ranges' of multiple problems. The question and the answer are copied verbatim below:

NPR: It's not a hill to climb; you've got a mountain range and then another mountain range and then another mountain range. How are you going to do that?

Mueller: We're doing our utmost. We have worked night and day to find solutions. Not only technical solutions. It's a lot of work for the lawyers, and for the press department.

I guess employees should feel honoured that he is not only considering 'technical solutions', particularly as technology was not at fault in the first place. What the lawyers and the press department will do to bring about the kind of changes that are clearly necessary is, to say the least, a mystery. The mind boggles.

Humour, honesty and hard work

Let me be very clear that the above examples do not mean that values cannot be properly made to live and work in an organisation. But as the Board Agenda survey tells us, top management focus on values is not a priority and hence the incidents outlined above are not uncommon. Of course, there are fine companies and organisations that take great care to ensure that from both the moral and management perspectives their value system, implicit or explicit, works well for all. And let's not forget that the larger the organisation the more difficult this is and influencing the micro-behaviours of say 100,000 employees through values is a non-trivial task and that's exactly why it needs to be high on the board's agenda.

However, for you starting out the easiest and most practical way to think about this is to observe the person you will be reporting to and the people in the department that you will belong to. They above all will determine the quality of your experience as an employee. Even in organisations where the values are ignored or limply supported at the top, great leaders and managers often can and do implement and live them in their own department.

I once met a manager who told me his company had three values. When I asked him what they were he could name and explain them on the spot. The three Hs they called them: Humour, Honesty and Hard work. The messages he explained were clear to all. Have fun and enjoy your work, be straight in all matters and get stuck in. When I enquired where they came from he said, "That's what the boss is like and he likes to hire people with these qualities." He said there were no brochures or presentations in existence about these values. He could remember them being written on a flip chart once but since then they simply exist and are on display every day, in the behaviour of the management.

Plastic values are harmful and need to be cleaned up

He thankfully never mentioned the most popular means of inculcating an organisation with its values. That is to have them printed on a plastic credit card sized square that fits in your wallet or purse. A lot of organisations do this. What is the expectation in requesting employees to carry around a proclamation of their company's values in their wallets? Might it be to ensure that they don't forget them? Should they pull them out and recite them before going to sleep? I really can't come up with a good reason as to why they would do this. But I can say with some certainty that if you want to cheapen what is meant to be a major cornerstone of the strategy of the organisation, i.e. how employees work together and interact with their customers, then print it on plastic and distribute it to your employees by the tens of thousands. That will for sure do the trick.

Proceed with care

Despite the awkward and expensive 'cultural' problems we have discussed, the employer branding people persist in touting the values of driven, socially responsible organisations dedicated to saving the planet whilst simultaneously providing simply awesome places to work. If anything, it has become the main selling point for attracting new employees. Social media is positively top heavy with whooping, high-fiving project teams, casually dressed selfie joining CEOs and barista directed office coffee stations. One can only wonder when any work gets done at all in modern organisations.

The average 21-year-old potential employee could be forgiven for thinking that his/her working life will be a hug-a-day love-in, with amazing colleagues and cuddly bosses. Whether it's on social media or the company website, what you are seeing here is branding with a capital B. A sales pitch. A cold call supported by some of the most sophisticated technology on the planet, all aimed at enticing you to become part of a selection process and in the wider sense to enhance the public perception of the organisation in question.

Be careful. Think of it like you are trying on a dress in a boutique. The sales assistant will inevitably at some point say, "You look amazing." Of course, the consequences of believing the schtick from a sales assistant is a great deal less serious than choosing a job based on the slick videos and high-definition photos of a workplace that exists only in the wildest fantasies of the employer branding people.

But the online stuff can be very seductive. Sometimes it all makes me wish I was 20 again. Or maybe not. The fact is that the other side of this discussion is not quite as rosy as the images on social media would have us believe. All the lights from employee surveys are flashing red. It appears that more people are alienated from their companies and colleagues than at any time in history. Stress, disengagement and insecurity stalk the world of work. Amy Adkins at Gallup reports that "millennials are the least engaged generation at work." Is the social media window dressing simply a reaction to the plethora of negative news about engagement and commitment at work and the inept attempts to make corporate cultures function? There is surely a connection.

All that glitters

The following anecdote is somewhat prescient:

An HR manager was tragically knocked down by a bus and killed. Her soul arrived at the Pearly Gates, where St Peter welcomed her. "Before you get settled in," he said, "we have a little problem... you see, we've never had an HR manager make it this far before and we're not really sure what to do with you." "Oh, I see," said the woman, "can't you just let me in?" "Well, I'd like to," said St Peter, "but I have higher orders. We're instructed to let you have a day in Hell and a day in Heaven, and then you are to choose where you'd like to go for all eternity." "Actually, I think I'd prefer Heaven," said the woman. "Sorry, we have rules..." at which St Peter put the HR manager into the downward bound lift.

As the doors opened in Hell, she stepped out on to a beautiful golf course. In the distance was a country club; around her were many friends, past fellow executives, all smartly dressed, happy, and cheering for her. They ran up and kissed her on both cheeks, and they talked about old times. They played a perfect round of golf and afterwards went to the country club where she enjoyed a superb steak and lobster dinner. She met the Devil (who was rather nice) and she had a wonderful night telling jokes and dancing. Before she knew it, it was time to leave. Everyone shook her hand and waved goodbye as she stepped into the lift.

The lift went back up to Heaven where St Peter was waiting for her. "Now it's time to spend a day in Heaven," he said. So, she spent the next 24 hours lounging around on clouds, playing the harp and singing, which was almost as enjoyable as her day in Hell. At the day's end St Peter returned. "So," he said, "you've spent a day in Hell, and you've spent a day in Heaven. You must choose between the two." The woman thought for a second and replied, "Well, Heaven is certainly lovely, but I actually had a better time in Hell. I choose Hell." Accordingly, St Peter took her to the lift again and she went back down to Hell.

When the doors of the lift opened, she found herself standing in a desolate wasteland covered in garbage and filth. She saw her friends dressed in rags, picking up rubbish and putting it in old sacks. The Devil approached and put his arm around her. "I don't understand," stuttered the HR manager, "the other day I was here, and there was a golf course, and a country club. We ate lobster, and we danced and had a wonderful happy time. Now there is just a dirty wasteland of garbage and all my friends look miserable." The Devil simply looked at her and smiled, "Yesterday we were recruiting you, and today, you're staff."

How to avoid falling into Hell!

1. 'The smell of the place'

The late Professor Sumantra Ghoshal when referring to organisations used to talk about what he called 'the smell of the place'. He often told a story of growing up in Kolkata (Calcutta) in India and eventually becoming a professor at INSEAD, one of the world's leading business schools near Paris. After spending some time at the beautiful campus at INSEAD, he perceived a difference in the quality of the air between the woods of Versailles and the streets of Kolkata. He pointed out that the air smelt somehow sweeter in Versailles than in the great city of Kolkata and used the notion of 'the smell of the place' as a means of representing and evaluating the culture of companies.

As a professor of Strategy, he would be invited by CEOs and their teams to help them think through their strategy, ways to approach their markets, new business models and so on. He would deliberately turn up early for these appointments and spend the extra time he had sitting in reception. There he would sit and observe and in effect assess 'the smell of the place'. He would observe the people coming and going. Were they energised, were they smiling? Did the receptionist make people feel welcome? Was the reception, which is of course the first point of contact for everyone who enters the company headquarters, warm, welcoming and stimulating? If so then great, if not, then what chance that the rest of the organisation will be any different? Rumour had it that he could pretty much guess the future financials of the company based on his observations in the reception.

Sniffing the air in reception

When you go for your interview try to arrive early. Thirty minutes should be enough. Sit in reception and check out the comings and goings. Soak it up and try to figure out who's who among the passers-by. If you are lucky one of the big bosses will pass through and you will have a chance to check her out. Does she greet the receptionist, does she stop and chat with people, is she approachable, does she carry her own bag? Does she look happy, sad, stressed, in a hurry, calm, relaxed – whatever? Also, if you get a chance go to the canteen or dining area as well and get a feel for the mood. Is there a buzz in the place? Try the food if you can. Is it good? Do the people who prepare and serve it care about the quality and their customers?

If you are visiting the headquarters, then check out the people who work there. Are they all locals or do they represent the global footprint of the company? The HQ of a company should be a microcosm of the world where they sell their products and their employee base. Pay attention also to how people dress. What does the dress code signify? An adherence to conformity or does it express a sense of individuality and freedom? A famous car manufacturer once boasted of having an inordinate number of engineers working on the cars' door handle because that was the first thing a potential buyer touched. Makes a lot of sense. The reception of an organisation is the first point of contact for customers, partners and potential employees like yourself. Don't underestimate the learning opportunity it presents.

2. Punctuality

Anyway, I'm a consultant and my consultant karma has developed a certain flexibility and stoical tolerance in its DNA. I expect to be kept waiting and I fully expect that schedule changes will affect me. And that's fine, I'm a specialist temporary employee who won't always fit into the cadence and schedule of the company I serve. The expectation is that I'll adjust accordingly and of course I do. Your situation will be somewhat different as you will be joining what is in effect an operational system as a member. So, if your appointment was at 11.00am and it was 11.20am before you were collected from the reception that's generally not a good sign. If you hear statements like "Our meeting overran and that's not unusual…" or "It's always hectic around here…" or "Mr Brown will be here shortly, his boss just called from Singapore…", you are seeing symptoms of what could well be a toxic, firefighting culture.

But of course, it's a matter of degree; appointments can run late, and nobody is looking for perfection. The important thing for you is to try and work out if you are experiencing an exceptional situation or the everyday standard way of working. If of course you are applying at a startup or a very new and growing company, it may simply be signs of an organisation that's still finding its feet. In this case the energy will be different and there will be a sense of adventure rather than resignation in the air. Time is a precious commodity in organisational life. Failure to manage it will surely reflect the culture and the leadership approach. Oddly enough I rarely if ever see punctuality as an espoused organisational value, I wonder why?

3. The annual report

When you are whiling away some time in reception figuring out 'the smell of the place' you will probably come across a copy of the annual report on the ubiquitous glass table. This can be a treasure trove of information. These things occupy a sacred place at the higher echelons of corporate life and tend to focus on the 'organisational myth', i.e. the romanticised ideal of what the company could be. If, as the survey mentioned earlier, boards don't really put much effort into developing and sustaining a positive culture, you can't say that about the annual report. It's normally overflowing with glossy pictures of board members as a group and individually sporting forced grins and often looking as comfortable as a bunch of polar bears on a beach.

Check out the pictures. Does the management team truly reflect the employee base of the company and indeed its customer demographic? What's the make-up of the team? Can you identify with anyone in the group? In short, do you feel you fit in? It's also popular these days to include photos and short job descriptions of the people who work at varying levels of the company. These can be informative, but few companies have managed to make them look authentic and real. Look at the financials, get a feel for the strategy. Read the statements made by the CEO and the senior team and you may get the basis of some great questions that you can ask at your interview. Nobody really expects job applicants to have read the annual report.

4. The physical working environment

The big discussion over the past 30 years regarding office space was whether you will be sitting in an open plan office, a smaller office shared with two or three others or an individual office. The architecture reflects and indeed helps determine the culture.

As a newbie it's extremely unlikely that you will have an individual or even small shared space. It's most likely to be open plan. Open plan offices were originally intended to enhance communication by removing barriers. Whilst it seems a good intuitive move, not everyone liked it. Some people love the buzz of the open plan setup, but the inherent noise and distraction has always been a bone of contention. But with people now regularly wearing headphones at work this has become less of a complaint. So even the most extreme introverts can find peace there.

We all have our preferences. But do try to consider your proximity to your colleagues and those you work closely with, to the toilets and particularly to windows and doors. Don't underestimate the importance of being comfortable with your space and the effect it will have on your productivity and your relationship with your colleagues.

Finally, find out the attitude of the company to home working. Many people shy away from the following two questions regarding time and space at work. Firstly, the policy and the opportunity to work from home, and secondly, the policy or support the company offers in terms of childcare. If these issues are important to you then address them. A well-organised approach to these issues is a sign that the company is interested in both your level of productivity and your comfort and wellbeing. Keep in mind that you may have to ask at an interview if you can have a quick walk through the office space where you will be working.

5. Our people are our greatest asset

If you come across the above sentence in the annual report or indeed anywhere else, I think it's best to politely make your excuses and head for the exit. Maybe you should carry a plastic or airline sick bag with you to the interview in case someone hits you with this statement. That's all I have to say about that.

Summary

Great companies and great employers find it difficult to hide their greatness. It's in the air in reception and on the faces of their employees. Above all they care about the little things. They don't have to plaster it all over HD screens or colour posters or sexy sounding initiatives to convince you of their greatness. So, take care and observe carefully. The truly authentic organisations are normally soft spoken and reserved.

- Culture is like the weather. It's ever-present and it can be bright and sunny or cold and dreadful. Make sure you are selecting an employer with more of the former.

- Culture tends not to be the first thing that top management want to deal with. We have seen the consequences of that. Things are changing but much too slowly.

- The reception and annual report are great places to get a feel for the organisation. Base some of your interview questions on what you observe and discover.

- Employer branding is very often a means of putting lipstick on a pig. The more companies crow about how wonderful and ethical they are the less you should expect it to be so.

- If someone offers you a plastic card with a list of values on it ask them what they have done with theirs. Try not to be tempted to tell them.

- Check out the company and the leadership as extensively as you can. Get the smell of the place before you commit.

CHAPTER FOUR

Change, Transformation Or Whatever They Are Calling It This Week

"Nothing so undermines organisational change as the failure to think through the losses that people face."

William Bridges

Almost without exception we are encouraged to embrace change. From internet memes to the latest leadership guru, change is almost always portrayed as something we should be all be on-board with. And those who resist change are often portrayed as being uncooperative, disruptive or as people who simply don't get it.

**THIS IS UTTER NONSENSE
SO PLEASE DON'T BELIEVE IT.**

Of course, it serves all of us well to have an open mind and to be receptive to what's new, different and challenging, both at work and in the world in general. But this is not a matter of simply raising your hand to everything that comes your way in the corporate world without giving due consideration to both the quality of the idea and the efficacy of its implementation plan.

Change is pretty much like everything else in life: too little of it is not good and too much of it can be dangerous. In the former case not enough can leave us stranded in organisational models and career paths that are well past their sell by date. Equally, too much of it can be damaging. It can be too frequent, confusing, poorly thought through and, if organisations are not careful, become the default response to every challenge that appears on the horizon.

This seems to be the situation for many organisations today and more importantly for the people who work in them. To describe change in organisations today as a cliché would not suffice. In organisational life the word itself has taken on almost mystical qualities as a panacea for meaningful action (look at us we are doing something!). You may also notice that some organisations have tried to spice up their change efforts by not actually using the word change. As if calling it 'transformation' was somehow going to be the killer app in getting a better outcome.

After the global financial crisis that began in 2008, we constantly heard that financial institutions needed a change in their cultures. Entire forests were felled to produce colour posters on values, leadership principles and other such nonsense to try and convince employees, customers and regulators that those who manage our money were somehow on the cusp of a miraculous transformation and that the days of building Ponzi schemes with their customers' money was over. Websites promised employees integrity and authenticity and pushed lines like 'our employees are our greatest asset' ad nauseam. One well-known bank actually produced a list of 13 'values' they expected their employees to live up to. An exceptional memory wasn't one of them.

As a young person starting their career you will be stepping into an organisation that will most probably be wrestling with the challenges of change. This chapter is designed to prepare you for that reality. We will introduce a model that will help you better understand what can be a very complex process. We will dive deep into change with a focus on how it may look from your standpoint i.e. the front line. We will then debate what constitutes good change that you should be happy to go with, and poorly thought through change that you should be wary of.

Turn right half a mile before you get there

Charles Handy, the Irish social philosopher, seeks to explain the dilemma of the speed and pervasiveness of change facing business today by relating the following story.

He once took a car journey from Dublin to the town of Avoca in County Wicklow on the east coast of Ireland. Wicklow is famous for its mountains, sea views and natural beauty. To cross the mountains, you must navigate narrow roads. Becoming unsure if he was driving in the right direction, he stopped to ask an old man the way. The conversation went as follows:

"Could you please tell me the best way to get to Avoca?"

"For sure, and it's easy. You go straight ahead up this hill for a mile or so until you get to a stream with a bridge over it; on the other side of it you'll see Davy's bar, you can't miss it, it's painted bright red."

"OK, I've got that, straight up then down the hill until I get to Davy's bar."

"Exactly, and then half a mile before you get to Davy's bar you turn right and that will take you to Avoca."

This tale neatly sums up the challenge of leading an organisation in the changing world of the 21st century where the key leadership skill would appear to be the ability to see around corners.

One observer provided the following apt description: *"Large scale organisational change is like replacing an engine on a Boeing 747 at 35,000 feet without losing altitude (degrading standards / service/quality) or spooking passengers (customers). During the process pilots (management) profess full control; cabin staff (employees) operate on a business as usual basis while engineers (change agents) work on the wing as F16s (the competition) buzzing the plane, intent on shooting it down."*

So, whilst we can and should be critical of poorly managed change, we ought to maintain a certain level of empathy with those in charge, given the extraordinary nature of the challenge.

Eating cold pizza at midnight

Companies have gone through some very visible changes in recent years. Not that long ago, many companies boasted exclusive executive toilets where only top management could go, men wore suits and ties and few women or minorities were to be seen in decision-making positions. And most of all, people in those organisations pretty much had a job for life. Whilst dress codes have relaxed and jobs for life have disappeared (maybe there's a connection), and whilst inclusiveness has made a lot of progress, we can't say that every organisation has mastered that challenge.

The very notion of change is, of course, dependent on reaching a state of equilibrium where the status quo is maintained for a significant period before the transition to the new state gets underway. Today for many managers and employees a period of stability appears to be a rare occurrence with many organisations being in a state of almost permanent change. A manager recently observed to me that "things are pretty good at the moment as we haven't had a new organisational chart so far this month." Yes, that's how bad it can get.

What really matters for you is to remain aware of just how competent the organisation is at providing a workplace where the management of change is not 100% dependent on the 'passion' or 'flexibility' or 'commitment' of the employees. Watch out for leaders who play that card, or you may find yourself eating cold pizza in the office at midnight in order to prove your flexibility and commitment to some overworked, poorly led and fearful boss.

You may be surprised to learn that some managers still regard working incredibly late and not seeing much of their families as a badge honour and they expect their employees to feel the same way. You would be making a massive mistake if you went along with that behaviour.

If you do walk into a job where change is a constant, then it's helpful to be able to build an understanding of what's happening. What's the scale of the change, what's the reasoning behind it? If you can grasp that then you will be able to figure out what's going on around you and how you should best react.

Change needs an energy source, a destination and a plan

Professor Michael Beer at Harvard has produced a wonderfully realistic way of understanding change. In short it consists of analysing change using his (D x M x I > C- Cost of Change) method.

The D here = Dissatisfaction. Who is dissatisfied with the status quo and is demanding change? The premise being that trying to impose change on happy people may not work. So, a certain level of readiness and impatience with the status quo should be present in order to energise the process.

The M = Model of the Future. Given that we are dissatisfied enough to desire and drive change, what might the destination look like? People will only follow if they can get a glimpse of a destination which is better and more attractive than the current one. (Without being political the Brexit process in Britain suffered greatly from the lack of a clear M.)

The I = the Implementation plan. So, what's the plan to take us to the new future and what's the sequence of events as we move forward? And finally, the benefits of the change must be greater than the costs of change. These can be economic, relational, motivational etc.

These four pieces of the puzzle have a multiplication relationship (D x M x I > C - Cost of Change) and therein lies its real power.

That's a pretty scant explanation of Beer's model but it does provide you with ideas for evaluating the change around you and gives you the basis to ask some very relevant questions. For instance, "Where is the impulse for this change coming from?" will help you get a handle on the management thinking for initiating the change. "What will the organisation look like when we have done this?" will give you an idea of the envisioned future and "What's the plan and what's our part and what are the costs involved?" may elicit the tangible steps necessary to get it done. Vague or nebulous answers to these questions may reveal that perhaps the process has not been that well thought through.

The received wisdom is that most change programmes do not deliver on their promises. McKinsey report that about 30% deliver on the goals set out at the start of the journey so there's about a 70% chance that you will experience some duds. Just make sure that you are not collateral damage.

Change can be brilliant, highly effective and life affirming

Let's focus on the 30% that are the success stories and expand the picture a bit. Jan Carlzon enacted extraordinary change at SAS Airlines in the 1980s and his work is still seen as a model of how to drive change by empowering staff at the front lines in a brilliantly creative way. He was one of the few who took empowerment directly to the employees who interacted with customers every day. He gave them licence to act and make decisions by giving them what became known as the 'little red book' that they could carry in their pocket. This graphical guide to actions that they were encouraged to take without asking for permission from a supervisor was transformational. Here the employees were not the consumers or indeed victims of change but the drivers of the entire process.

John Legere as CEO transformed T-Mobile in the US into a market leader with his incredible focus on both his staff and customers. He even dressed and cut his hair like his much younger employees and even spent time answering customer calls with them. Through this he brought not just energy but a relentless approach to putting the customer first in a service industry. Like Carlzon he included and engaged his workforce and created extraordinary success for all his stakeholders. Change in these cases was not embodied in some high-flying strategy but in engaging the contribution of every employee.

Working in either of these organisations and indeed the many others that manage change well would have been both educational and fun.

But it would be a mistake to focus only on organisational change when looking to build a greater understanding of the world of change. Extraordinary social and political changes happen at an ever-increasing rate. These often overturn ways of thinking and acting that have been unquestionable for centuries. The peaceful approaches to political change as espoused by people like Gandhi, King and Mandela have shown what's possible in a world that simply could not comprehend the approach as these movements began. Social changes in the area of LGBT and gender rights were not even considered by those in power in the very recent past. Talent is increasingly being freed up to meet opportunity irrespective of who you are or where you come from and that can only be a good thing. Most, if not all, of these changes appeared impossible at the time of their inception.

People used to smoke on aeroplanes

That's true. At check-in you would have the choice of a smoking or non-smoking seat. The no-smoking signs would be extinguished when the plane reached cruising altitude. On long-haul flights committed smokers used that time to prepare to light up. They would have their cigarettes and lighters or matches at the ready. Some would already have a cigarette or pipe in their mouth and would be staring transfixed at the sign waiting and praying for it to go dark. Within a nanosecond of that happening flames would meet cigarette and the whole back of the plane would soon be covered by a cloud of smoke. This practice only came to an end in the late 1990s, with only a small fraction of countries and airlines still permitting on-board smoking today.

Naked flames, clouds of smokes, and flight attendants serving food and drinks through the haze with people eating, drinking and smoking at 36,000 feet. Today it's almost impossible to imagine for someone who has never experienced it. Back then it was unremarkable, legal, normal behaviour. Then changing attitudes to health, to safety and to the rights of non-smokers made smoking on planes not only disappear but appear simply astonishing that it was ever allowed in the first place. But if you had said to someone at the start of this process that no one would be permitted to smoke on planes five years later they would have said you were crazy, that it would be impossible and would never, ever be accepted. Lessons from life like these are largely ignored by those who design corporate change programmes.

Of course, since then the smoking ban has been extended to include practically all workspaces and many public places. These changes were imposed by governments at the behest of concerned individuals and groups despite enormous resistance by vested interests. It could be argued that in this case government legislation left little choice but to go with the change, but acceptable change does not happen purely through a top-down command. If that worked, and it rarely does, then change would be easy.

In any case, I would bet that the average CEO has more than enough power to enact serious beneficial change in his organisation with outcomes as powerful and thrilling to his people as the above examples. The question is if he is willing to embrace real change. Maybe he could take some inspiration from outside the turgid box of corporate change processes and instead of seeing change as a mechanical process see it for what it is, i.e. an opportunity to excite and engage the entire workforce in what could be the ride of their lives.

Change at the front line

OK, back to reality. Some time back I was asked to make an intervention to help get a global team in the services arena back on track. They had lost their mojo and needed to rethink their structure, strategy and communications. The team leader who requested the intervention gave me the background and we discussed the interview protocol I was planning for the team members and various options for action. He then went on to explain that this intervention was "a stand-alone temporary rescue mission" as he termed it.

As we talked, he revealed that the company was undergoing a large scale 'behind the scenes' change effort which had not yet been made known to the participants and that I, under no circumstances, should discuss it with them. When I requested some details re this programme so that I could at least 'secretly' align with its main concepts he could not help me as he had not been given the details himself. He had simply been told it was in progress and all would be revealed in the fullness of time.

Whilst I was trying to conceptualise an approach that would somehow be helpful to the team in this unusual situation, he dropped his final bombshell. He said, "One last thing you should know, I'll be leaving the company myself and I'll announce it at the first team workshop." Naturally, I was stunned by this revelation and was at a loss to imagine just how to be of help both to him and his team. I also felt that I needed to get to know this person a bit better to truly understand the scope of the assignment and indeed the current state of the team at a deeper level.

Was this team leader a devious, opportunistic manager? A slick corporate surfer who could survive and thrive in any chaos and move on at the right moment? What was the real reason he wanted this intervention if he was moving on himself? Was he endeavouring to use me in some way to apply a sticking plaster of sorts to an already defunct and dysfunctional group?

As we continued our discussions it became clear that he absolutely was not. I soon discovered that he was a caring, smart, committed man who was close to tears as he explained that he simply could not sustain a decent team environment for his people in the face of what he termed "top-down, idiotic, reactive, piecemeal and unrelenting change." He was exhausted and not from working for his clients or exercising his strengths in a job that he loved but by the internal machinations of a leadership and organisation who saw a redrawing of the lines and a reshuffle of the boxes as the only 'safe' answer to every challenge that loomed on their business horizon. This approach was preferred to one where the employees involved could have been recruited and engaged in helping to implement the real meaningful change they wanted so badly and were more than qualified to enact.

The team leader explained that he wanted me to at least provide a space for discussion for team members both on the group and individual level where they could vent their frustrations, redesign their work in so far as that was possible, and help them become a more united and cohesive group as they tackled the challenges ahead. Whilst this was an exceptional situation for me it has in the meantime become more and more common. Incessant top-down change is pushing great managers and employees to their very limits.

Of course, whatever business you work in you will at some point be affected. So, what do we do about it? How should you prepare for the inevitable change you will encounter as you progress in your career and how will you differentiate the good from the awful?

Change you may have to tolerate if not exactly embrace

In some situations, there really is no choice but to go with the change being imposed. If your company has been acquired or indeed divested, then you have little choice. If a restructuring happens with people losing their jobs and departments being amalgamated there won't be much you can do.

Beware of downsizing where the salami slicer strategy is used. Let`s say the company is set to lose 1,000 jobs. Management then announce that each department is required to get rid of a certain number, for example 10%. Management like to pretend this is a 'fair' way to implement the changes. It's not and all it really shows is that they really don't know the value drivers in the company either from a people performance or a team/process perspective. It's normally the coward's way out in the guise of 'everyone is being treated the same'. Make your choice, go or stay, that is if you survive the salami slicer. I guess you know what I would do.

Be healthily sceptical of the following attempts at change

1. The new manager shows up with a bagful of ideas!

A new manager arrives and immediately wants to make an impression. Managers like to be seen to be doing something, particularly if they are new. They will very likely have been coached to empower their people and will at least be trying to keep their fingers out of the operational work. So many are faced with the dilemma of what to do with themselves. Some organise more meetings, and some arrive with a palette of ideas that they saw working in their last department or previous company, and they decide that you and your colleagues deserve the benefit of this wisdom. He may also have recruited one of his favourite people from his last job to help him implement.

This falls into the category of 'shaking things up' and it's meant to transmit the following messages. Firstly, there is a new Sheriff in town so watch out and secondly, that he's a guy who gets things done.

Inherently, there is nothing wrong with new people bringing new ideas. But a knee-jerk response to a new position can be dangerous. The real test is if he really has had a good look at what you are doing and gets the buy-in and support from you and the team to do it differently. Don't wait to be asked. Offer your help. Tell him you and the team would be happy to join in and share your ideas. If he's not interested, then you can conclude that this change may not be for you.

2. Large-scale organisational change that mentions becoming number one

Vast sums of money have been spent on 'change programmes' that never impact the business. They fly high above the clouds and are manifested in posters and booklets and cards and 'keynotes' and have as much effect on the culture as weather forecasters have on the weather. Robert Schaffer wrote an HBR article entitled 'Successful Change Programmes Begin with Results' where he beautifully highlights this problem.

Referring to a Quality Improvement Change programme at a US financial services company, he writes:

"The programme trained hundreds of employees and communicated its intent to thousands more. At the end of two years of costly effort the programme consultants summarised progress. 'Forty-eight teams up and running. Two completed Quality Improvement stories. Morale of the employees regarding the process very high to date.' They did not report any bottom-line performance improvements, because there were none."

Schaffer goes on to categorise change programmes into two main areas: what he terms *activity-based* programmes which are characterised by nebulous goals, large investments and a top-down approach. On the other hand, he highlights the advantages of focused change with tangible goals. These he termed *results focused*. These are owned at the front line and targeted on making immediate improvements to the business. These results-focused efforts build on each other in a way that delivers continuous results and builds confidence and ambition in the process. This is the kind of change programme you want to be involved with and to make a contribution to.

3. Anything that has 'culture change' or 'cost out' in the title

One way of understanding culture is to see it as being 'largely determined by the worst behaviour a CEO is willing to tolerate'. So, if she ignores bad behaviour, particularly at a senior level, then this behaviour will become 'acceptable' and will be replicated by others in the organisation. The irony of this statement is that the expense and disruption of any 'culture change' programme she may want to start could be avoided if she paid attention to rooting out the bad behaviour in her management team and acted on the outcomes of employee engagement surveys and other such people-centred data as a real priority. So when I hear the words 'culture change' from senior management and the demands that employees behave this way or that way, I seriously wonder if they have grasped even the most basic understanding of what their roles as change leaders really entail.

The idea of naming a programme 'Cost Out' is, if anything, even scarier than calling it 'Culture Change'. At least the term culture is somewhat distant from the daily existential concerns of the average employee. Cost hits close to home because when the programme gets going, headcount or FTEs, which is basically accounting slang for people who are full-time employees, may well show up on the cost side of the ledger. In effect people could end up working to make themselves redundant. Imagine having a manager whose understanding of team spirit, employee motivation and indeed the relationship between people and productivity is so negligible that he would proudly announce a programme called 'Cost Out'.

Of course, money needs to be saved and budgets managed, it a fact of organisational life in any industry. But how you name it, position it and discuss it with employees is what makes it effective. The real test is the following question. Is investment in the organisation and the potential of its people as clear and focused and trumpeted to any degree with the same fanfare as cost out? I'll let you ponder on that as you gain experience in your new company.

Change that you should hug, embrace and be excited about

4. You are informed, invited, involved and engaged

Imagine your manager calling your team together and making the following short speech which is very similar to one I once heard.

"Everybody, thanks for coming. As you are aware, as an organisation we are doing well. Our financial indicators are good, and the results of our last employee survey were largely positive, and we are working on the parts that need our attention. We make great products and serve our customers well and I'm proud of the contribution that we as a department make to our overall success. We all know that change is a permanent feature of our lives here and that we like to engage with the new demands our customers have at the earliest possible stage. That means we need to look at ourselves on occasion and figure out what changes we may have to make internally to meet these external demands. So, this is about us looking internally at the work we do and identifying areas that perhaps don't add so much value. Let me tell you a short story to illustrate this.

"A long time ago, I think it was about 1948, when the current Queen of Great Britain was a princess she was on tour in South Africa and had dinner with the then prime minister of that country overlooking Cape Town harbour. Compared to him she was very young and of course finding conversation topics wasn't that easy. The story goes that during one silence the princess spotted a dolphin in the harbour and she asked the prime minister, 'How many dolphins have you got here?' He didn't know but asked an aide and eventually an answer came back to the question. I'm unsure what that answer was but apparently the counting of dolphins went on until about 1999 in Cape Town harbour.

"Processes get stuck, habits get ingrained and we don't see these things unless we actively look for them. Our task in small groups for the next 40 minutes is to find where we may be counting dolphins in our department. In other words, are we issuing reports no one ever reads, are we spending too much time on X or Y, are we doing repeat work? You are the people who can surface all of this so let's go hunting dolphins."

This approach respects and trusts the knowledge and expertise of the team members and puts them in control of their own work and its outputs. Imagine having the chance to do this a couple of times per year and its effects on motivation and productivity. A simple, inclusive and free intervention.

Summary

We must accept that large-scale change is a non-trivial challenge. Companies could and should take inspiration from the social and political changes around us, instead of sticking rigidly to the corporate toolbox. Change in organisations should be implemented in an inclusive fashion where employees at all levels are informed and engaged. The change model gives us a means of understanding the big picture and developing the right questions. Beware of imposed or knee-jerk change where your input is not asked for and accept the times where you won't have any choice but to accept what's happening. To participate in well-managed change can be a challenging, exciting and wonderful learning experience. Embrace it.

- You don't have to embrace all change. Just remember that. It's an evaluation and a choice you will likely have to make more than once in your career.

- Do keep in mind that not everyone can see around corners, so please keep an open mind, and an empathic heart for those trying to balance the organisational change with that of the world outside.

- Learn the right questions to ask. Consider the reasoning behind the change, the planned destination and the efficacy of the plan that's going to make it fly.

- There is much that the corporate world can learn from change outside the door. Stay in touch with the social and political world of change. The company is part of that world and has much to learn.

- Sometimes you won't have a choice. Change will arrive and there won't be one question you can ask or one thing you can do. All you will be able to do is observe, evaluate and decide what's good for you.

- Change is a promise of better times ahead, if that's not happening then it may be time to move on. Do try and have at least one great change learning experience, or better still when you are CEO make sure you provide that exhilarating experience for your people.

CHAPTER FIVE

It's Team Time And Now You're A Player

"It's better to learn the lessons during the game than talk about it afterwards."

Liverpool FC manager Jürgen Klopp to BT Sport – October 2019

Joining a team is almost a certainty when you begin your new job. Rather than explain that you are in the department of Global Widget Planning or whatever, most people use the simple team word to describe their work unit. The name also conveys more of a feeling of togetherness and colour and excitement than the boring old word department. Does that really make any difference? Well maybe. I have never run a 'department-building event' but the corporate world is replete with team-building events and they are available in an amazing range of approaches, activities and objectives. I have seen events on board ships, in forests climbing through trees, hill walking and indeed fire-walking expeditions, paint-ball mini wars, psychologists using a myriad of team profilers; I have even seen a team-building take place in an open air circus on the beach. Swinging on the trapeze was the main challenge on that occasion.

In addition to exciting bonding opportunities, teams can make for a wonderful working environment. Well led and functioning teams can make you feel you really are part of a group effort instead of being a solitary drone. All of us will at some point in our lives have felt the positive vibes of belonging to a group of people striving to achieve something together. It's a brilliant feeling.

Sport is leading the way

Of course, many if not most of these experiences will have involved sport. The word team is borrowed from the sporting world and how the development of sporting teams has progressed in recent years is simply astonishing. Today if you play for a professional football team you are supported, measured, coached in ways that only a short time ago would have been deemed science fiction. Barcelona FC will soon be producing personalised energy drinks for each player based on their personal physiological makeup and requirements. You, however, are going to be stuck with the coffee machine and if your company has caught the 'cost out' religion then you'll probably have to pay for it as well.

A top-class football team is representing an enormous commercial enterprise, but you and your team are as well. You and your team are a vital part of the value created by your company for customers and indeed all stakeholders, so never underestimate your role. Whilst sporting team development has changed drastically with the application of science over the years, little has changed for company teams since Vance Packard, the US advertising guru, bemoaned the advent of the 'team man' in the 1950s US industry.

Team spirit and structure

The teambuilding events I alluded to are mainly aimed at improving 'team spirit' and morale, which is absolutely essential, and they can be brilliant and uplifting but their shelf life is very much dependent on what happens when you get back to the office. In my experience the real value-adding impact of these events can be best felt when this focus on spirit is combined with an equal focus on structure.

Let's look again at the world of football. The team spirit of football teams tends to be exemplified by feelings of camaraderie and loyalty the players feel for each other and their club and this, of course, gets amplified by their fans. But that is insufficient for football coaches, and coaches know that spirit alone on a football pitch does not get you where you want to go.

That's why one of the most constant refrains you will hear from football coaches to their teams is "keep your shape", i.e. stay in your allocated position and play the role allocated to you in the team. In other words, these teams have a deep and compulsory underlying structure or system. This combination is vital, as the shape/structure is the engine of performance whilst the spirit can be considered as the fuel providing the energy as well as the emotional 'glue' holding the members together.

Here's what I want you to take from this chapter. Firstly, that you gain a good general understanding of how teams function in organisations. Secondly, that collaboration, the very cornerstone of teamwork, can and does work and produces great outcomes for all concerned. Thirdly, a grasp of the fact that the act of collaboration can be twisted and used to create cover and camouflage for teammates who may be exploitative. We will dive deep into just one strategy that if you get it right will ensure you are not exploited or bullied and will enhance your ability to manage yourself and your team relationships effectively.

The tip of the spear

As we have seen, football coaches would never depend on spirit alone to keep the team winning, but I have seen lots of corporate managers and team leaders who opt for a yearly fun outing for the team and then wonder why their performance is substandard for the rest of the year. Teams are the main work units of modern organisations. They handle suppliers and customers, drive productivity and are the people at the very heart of creating value.

They are the tip of the spear of a commercial organisation yet team development all too often appears to be a random process dependent on the budget and the knowledge or indeed the willingness of the manager in question. Some teams work in one way because their manager read a certain book whilst others may have a totally different approach. Whilst there may be no one perfect way to run a team you would expect some level of consistency across an organisation, particularly given the extraordinary progress teams in the sporting area have made based on science-based interventions. The continuing lack of focus from organisational leadership regarding the key work unit of their operations is puzzling. So don't be surprised at the different approaches and levels of performance you will experience. However, one company really took the clear importance of team performance to heart and decided to invest in just how they could create consistently better performing teams. That was Google.

Project Aristotle @ Google

Google crunch data, and as a company are dedicated to the collection and dissemination of data, and they have plenty of it, most of it about the people who use their services. But of course, they also generate tons of internal data concerning their people, their business strategy and so on. A few years ago, they decided to turn their big data guns on themselves and began a project to look at just how their most successful teams function. They reached the following conclusions, most of them totally unsurprising, apart from one. That was that nowhere in the research did they find that technical skills were a big differentiator in making teams work well.

They concluded that teams perform well when they have members who can depend on each other, when they have structure and clarity, when their work has a real impact and when it is accompanied by a sense of meaning. All sounds like pretty standard stuff. However, in order to make the above aspects function, they highlighted one specific factor that must exist in the group. This they term 'psychological safety'. This was their primary finding and it's worth exploring a bit more.

Amy Edmondson at Harvard who has long researched this topic describes this as "having the shared belief that the team is safe for interpersonal risk taking" and that having "confidence that the team will not embarrass, reject or punish someone for speaking up." This they found was the key factor in distinguishing the best teams from the ordinary teams at Google. Easier said than done as Google freely admitted. But they have given a name to what good managers and team leaders have always known, that communication and empathy are the basis of great teamwork. But they wanted to get this into the bones of a very large organisation, or as they put it in Google terms 'into an algorithm they could easily scale'.

Maybe that sounds a bit techy for most of us but their effect on their colleagues was profound. Remember Google has a lot of computer geeks and engineers in their ranks and the fact that these findings came from a data-crunching exercise of course got their attention. By surfacing this issue, they created licence for people to address it and what was previously difficult to discuss suddenly found its legitimate place as a key factor in the success of the company.

If there is one skill you should focus on learning, it's the creation of this safety as well as the ability to be able to demand it from your superiors. We have discussed self-awareness in other chapters in this book. But take whatever steps you need to try and further develop your ability to understand and develop the ability to be an influencer in this respect in the team you join. Find a mentor, take a great profiler like the Birkman or anything from the Gallup organisation that will help you engage on this topic. You can be sure that if this thinking has permeated Google it will for sure be expected at a host of other companies. Be ready.

A really useful definition of the word team

Probably the best and most used definition of team comes from Katzenbach and Smith in their book *The Wisdom of Teams* (1994):

"A group of individuals with complementary strengths who are committed to a common purpose, performance goals and an approach for which they hold themselves mutually accountable."

The complementary strengths, for instance creativity and structure, will produce a combined effort greater than each individual one alone. But this effort must have direction and focus its energy on the purpose the team is committed to achieve in a measurable way. All pretty easy and clear. Then the last line talks of 'mutual accountability', that means you have a stake in me being successful in my job and I have a stake in making sure you get yours done with the best possible outcome. This is not an easy concept to structure and implement for most team leaders, but we will explore this in more depth in the chapter on meetings.

It's your job, your time, your space and you don't owe anybody anything

We will now focus on just one key aspect of team life that if you get right you will be arriving early, sharpening your strengths and skills, eating lunch in peace and heading home or to your favourite hotspot as planned and on time. That's a promise. Before we explore this 'must learn' strategy, let's just consider some more the compelling upsides of real collaborative teamwork.

The fundamental idea behind teamwork lies in the fact that groups in general produce better solutions than individuals and therefore create higher quality products and solutions. We know this. The simple act of bringing different perspectives together can magically transform the quality of decisions in groups. This is even possible when team members are not so familiar with the topic in question. In fact, inexperienced teams have been known to outperform individual experts in their area of expertise. So, two heads are better than one and three are better than two.

So why does this not happen every time and in every team? Steven Pinker in his book *Enlightenment Now* made the following statement on human interaction: "*Our cognitive, emotional and moral faculties are adapted to individual survival in an archaic environment...not to universal thriving in a modern one...*" In other words, in high-pressure situations people often revert to questionable behaviour and indeed downright bullying or deceit to get their own way or escape responsibility.

It's a fuzzy line between collaboration and exploitation

In the hubbub of a busy team day there can be a fine line between collaboration and exploitation. So how do you tell the difference and what can you do to ensure you don't get exploited or bullied? It's a serious issue. Jeffrey Pfeffer of Stanford University reports that 44% of nurses in the UK National Health Service had experienced bullying inside a 12-month period and as a result suffered from anxiety and depression. Despite having read the company's values statement that emphasised collaboration, and the leadership principles that talked of teamwork, sooner or later you will discover that the line between collaboration and exploitation was not very well defined at all.

Try to become a Viking once a day

Danish people live in what is very much an egalitarian society and they tend to be very direct and open. When Geert Hofstede did his famous cultural studies, the Danes scored lowest in the world on his Power Distance measure. This means that they regard power as more of a shared concept than simply a top-down one. In short that means that managers and employees can have very honest discussions and employees tend to voice their disagreement quite openly. In other words, they can say no to bosses and colleagues more often than employees in any other country.

If you cannot, when necessary, channel your inner Viking you can seriously spoil not just your team experience but your career and life in general. That is your ability to focus and to develop a filter that separates stuff that serves firstly you and secondly the team from stuff that doesn't. A principal part of that filter will be your ability to turn down requests from colleagues and even bosses and say the simple but often elusive word no.

I'm going to push you hard on this because it's a key topic. It really does not matter much how talented, educated or knowledgeable you are when you join a working team. In fact, if you have all of the above in abundance but lack what it takes to articulate the word no to your superiors, peers, clients or whoever, you will run the risk of turning your early experience of working in a team into a trip to the depths of Hell. If you are unable or unwilling to mouth the said word you will by default rewrite your job description from whatever it was meant to be into '*The person who willingly cleans up other people's crap*'. Then you will attract legions of the aforementioned people, as if you were wearing a Post-it on your forehead with your new job description written on it. What will then happen is that this will become your official job description, in so far as your boss and teammates will recognise this wonderful talent and pile more crap on you. In addition, you will get extremely good at cleaning up the crap and get worse at what you are meant to be doing.

The gravestone is dedicated to those who cannot say NO in large organizations. They bury their own career.

If you keep up this ridiculous behaviour long enough, it will be inscribed on your career tombstone. Insert your name above, close your eyes and see how it feels. If you take on too much you will end up not just overwhelmed but could end up in toxic one-sided work relationships. Suddenly someone else's inability to get their job done becomes your responsibility. And of course, these games are often played under the 'legal' cover of collaboration. Such cases are borderline bullying and you need to be wise to it. Try and build a set of reciprocal relationships inside the team from the start. Nothing is for free. A great reciprocal relationship goes way beyond mutual back scratching and is at the heart of highly productive collaboration.

'Independence is a prerequisite for interdependence'. I borrowed this statement from Steven Covey, the late American thinker and author. It means that true collaboration works when the contributors come from a place of certainty and confidence. In other words, when you are independently functioning and have your role under control and your work partner does as well then you both are in a much better position to truly collaborate. Your independence comes first. Keep that in mind.

The journey from no to yes

What does the word 'no' actually mean in the workplace and why are so many people so reluctant to use it? People tend to think that they won't be regarded as a team player, that they are uncollaborative and negative. In actual fact saying no simply demonstrates that you are focused, you have structured your time well and you are in control of your own schedule and energy. In other words, you are the dream employee. The ability to say a measured 'no' signifies your independence of mind, confidence and courage. When you have got that far then you are ready to really collaborate and create shared value with others.

Judith Sills summarises it as follows:

"No is a moment of clear choice. It announces, however indirectly, something affirmative about you. 'I will not sign' – because that is not my truth. 'I will not join your committee, help with your kids, review your project' – because I am committed to some important project of my own. 'Count me out' – because I'm not comfortable, not in agreement, not on the bandwagon. 'No, thank you' – because you might feel hurt if I turn down your invitation, but my needs take priority."

But let's be clear, collaboration is an absolute necessity in any organisation and always has been. It's impossible to get anything done on your own and most of the time the product or service you are producing is the result of the efforts of many people. But collaboration is a messy and ill-defined area of endeavour and whilst it's something many organisations and superiors trumpet loudly, they often do little to facilitate its implementation proactively in the workplace.

Sometimes it's simply a dog eat dog situation where the loudest and pushiest dominate the scene and bosses avoid having sensible team conversations about how to make it work. This results in overworked employees showing up in tears in his/her office and then instead of discussing how to collaborate, the discussion becomes one of who's right and who's wrong. In fairness to anyone managing a team, it is difficult to structure and control particularly in times of great change. However, it's at the heart of team leadership and not taking the time to plan and discuss just how to do this is negligent in the extreme.

Of course, there will be occasions when it is clearly necessary for everyone to join in immediately and get stuff done. Emergencies do happen and even with the best will in the world cannot always be avoided. But if your team-working life is an ongoing emergency and you are spending your time and energy on constant, unfocused firefighting, then you are no longer in charge of your own destiny and you may need to rethink your position. The fact is you are pretty much on your own when it comes to this aspect of your early working life and you are going to have to deal with it from the get-go. You can't always depend on the boss and don't for a moment imagine that you will always have super cool colleagues. You won't.

A 'Yes' is something you should not give away cheaply

According to James Altucher, the US investor and entrepreneur, Bill Murray the actor says "No" to most things. People ask him to act in a film; 99% of the time he says "No." People ask to take their picture with him. He says "No."

Altucher neatly illustrates a Bill Murray 'Yes' using the following story and I paraphrase:

One time he was in a cab for an hour and got talking to the cab driver. He asked the driver what he does when he's not driving a cab.

"I like to play the sax."

"How often do you practise?" Bill said.

"Not very often. Busy driving this cab."

"Where's the sax now?"

"In the trunk."

"Pull over," said Bill, "I know how to drive a car too. Get the sax."

Bill drove.

The cab driver sat in the back and played the sax.

That's a Bill Murray 'Yes'.

The point here is that your 'yes' is a precious gift to others and if you give it away too lightly, too freely, it will lose its value and you will lose part of your uniqueness as a person.

Understanding your yes from this perspective will demand that you regard your ability to say no as a non-trivial attitude and skill that will serve you well for the rest of your life. When you have fully internalised and practised this, your confidence will increase, and your demeanour will change accordingly.

Summary

Team-based work is probably here to stay and you experience many different teams throughout your working life. Gain some clarity on the structure of the team and your role inside of that. Don't be surprised at the wide variety of the understanding of the concept of teamwork you will encounter. The concept of psychological safety is a key. Make it an agenda item on your team meetings. Get your boss to openly not only address the issue but come up with a structure that really helps people understand how work can be shared in an equitable way and so that no one feels exploited. Be proactive in your dealing with your teammates and try to ensure that they understand firstly your role and secondly your boundaries.

- Teams are energised by spirit and organised by structure, and these two factors, nurtured and renewed on an ongoing basis, are key to successful team performance.

- You will encounter many different approaches to team development. Often, there is no shared team strategy in the company and it's dependent on each individual leader, budget, etc.

- Be very aware of your role, deliverables and area of responsibility. Agree these with the person in charge. Be equally aware of your interfaces and make sure that collaboration is balanced and reciprocal. Remember there will always be grey areas.

- Psychological safety is the basis for great cooperation and collaboration. If it exists, then meetings and interactions will be more spontaneous and genuine. If your boss cannot deliver on this, then you will have to create your own.

- Figure out what a good healthy collaborative working relationship feels like for you and ensure that you do something if things start getting toxic. Don't suffer in silence.

- Your understanding of and ability to appropriately use the words No and indeed Yes will prove to be a vital stepping-stone in developing both yourself and your career.

CHAPTER SIX

Meet The Meetings – A Truly Dysfunctional Family

"If you had to identify, in one word, the reason why the human race has not achieved, and never will achieve, its full potential, that word would be 'meetings'."

Dave Barry

Organisations are organic structures, they consist of living, breathing people. Let's pretend that an organisation is a person and its health is dependent on both its genetic history and its lifestyle. Does your organisation get enough sleep, does it take enough exercise, does it eat in a healthy way? Or is it a lazy, couch lounging, TV dinner consuming, screen gazing insomniac? If so, how could we get it to relax and shake off its ill-disciplined approach to organisational fitness?

Wherever the question regarding wellbeing comes up these days, mindfulness and yoga always appear to be part of the answer. Maybe, for a start at least, the organisation should take up yoga. Yoga instructors always tend to start with breathing and its importance to overall health. It's the only function of the autonomic nervous system that you can control and by doing so you gain an extraordinary amount of control over the state of your body. Practised regularly you can achieve serious long-term health benefits such as a greater ability to relax, more positive feelings, less stress, enhanced relationships, and so on. Imagine having these outcomes for the entire company simply through having the company learn to breathe.

Meetings are the organisation's opportunity to breathe. It gets to inhale and exhale through the process of multiple meetings. They can provide the opportunity for people to inhale new information, set new ideas in motion, celebrate the success of past projects and flood the team with the oxygen of optimism. Concluded projects, plans and strategies, frustrations, failures and mistakes can be discussed, exhaled and dispensed with. The organisation should be refreshed and rejuvenated through this constant and continual exchange. If, after all, communication is the oxygen of organisational life then meetings are, or at least should be, the lungs that power that process.

David Pearl in his wonderful book *Will There Be Donuts?* categorises meetings in an apt and humorous way. He gives great examples of meetings that have become organisational entities. For instance, he identifies the Wagner meeting, named after the German opera composer Richard Wagner, which like one of his operas appears to go on for ever. These are far too common in many companies. He nails what he calls the 'mushroom' meetings, which simply appear from nowhere and multiply rapidly whilst the 'Stonehenge' meeting is a relic that's always been there, but nobody really knows why. He captures the essence of how meetings can become habitual rituals and permanent fixtures in organisations. To some extent we can think of these as almost being genetically fixed in the DNA of the company as they can be desperately hard to shift.

This chapter is designed to help you to understand meeting structures in, for example, your team, i.e. the different kinds of meeting that exist and how they relate to each other (that is of course if they are structured at all). Then we will seek to help you understand the focus and objectives of each type of meeting and how and why they need to be differentiated from each other. We will discuss why meetings need names and how meetings without names can be confusing. Different types of meetings will be explored along with just how people often behave in meeting situations. And, as ever, I will add various tips for you that will enhance your meeting experience.

The organisation is gasping for breath

Managers and employees spend a huge percentage of their time in meetings. They happen night and day. They are big and they are small. They happen standing up or sitting down, in boardrooms and on building sites, on factory floors and both online and offline or indeed a mixture of both. They happen for a vast number of different reasons. Some are brilliantly planned and superbly structured and executed. Most are anything but and tend to be soul-sucking, energy-consuming, time-wasting nonsense which few people apart from the occasional masochist look forward to attending.

I know brilliant engineers for whom a fraction of a millimetre of inaccuracy in measurement on one of their engineering projects would be regarded as a personal affront. These same people are prepared to sit in on or even run meetings that have little focus, no structure, intangible goals and will finish hours after the agreed time and then only when participants have started eating the furniture. It's truly astonishing just how little organisations have learned about running meetings over the years.

As the new girl in town check out meeting attendees as they make their way to the appointed room. They often resemble children ambling along reluctantly to school. Any distraction will do. The coffee machine or water cooler makes a good place to observe from:

"What you up to Tom?"

"Nothing really, I just need a coffee before I go to that meeting…"

"What's it about then?"

"Something to do with the budget…but I'm not really sure…"

"Let's have lunch then, what time is it finishing?"

"Well John is running it so it might drag on, hell, I'm late… I'll call you."

What is going on? When are companies going to stop gasping for breath and learn to breathe? Surely the ability to organise a relatively simple function so vital to the effectiveness, not to mention health, of the company and its employees cannot be beyond the abilities of a modern organisation? Tragically it frequently is and it's incredibly important that you learn how to deal with the meeting culture you will encounter at work.

You get the big invitation

The word 'meeting' has an extraordinary power to both excite and terrify newly hired potential participants. "The CEO just invited me to a meeting…", "I have to represent my boss at the next meeting...", "I'm on the list for top team meeting…", "I have to make a presentation at the next team meeting…" These statements are normally gasped out by a slightly nauseous newbie whose colleagues look at her with a mix of jealousy and relief. Everyone is aware that it may be a chance to shine, to really show just how good you are, or conversely it could be a big-time opportunity to screw things up.

Billy Connolly, the Glaswegian comedian, used to tell a story that went something like this:

When I was nine years old, I was walking down a street in Glasgow with my grandfather and I saw a man coming towards us who was wearing a bandage on his head.

I asked, "Grandad, what do you think happened to that poor man?"

He answered, "Well son, I don't know exactly, but I will tell you one thing I am pretty sure about."

"What's that?"

"Well, I'll bet you that he was talking when he should have been listening."

Take Billy's advice and try to avoid having to wear the organisational equivalent of a bandage on your head around the office. Please curb your enthusiasm on getting the invitation to your first meetings. Prepare for whatever part has been allocated to you. Listen and tune into the vibe of the meeting you are attending, be modest and stay in learning mode.

Meetings need first names

I have been to lots of meetings. Meeting rooms in companies tend to have names that often reflect the various locations of the company. I have frequently sat in rooms called Vienna, Houston, London, Jakarta, Singapore, Berlin, etc., only to find the meeting I was attending remained nameless. At least I could locate the room where it was happening if not the point of the meeting.

Take away the name and all meetings start to look alike. This results in a recurring question that haunts many people in large companies. What's this meeting all about and why in God's name am I here? Meetings that are simply referred as 'the meeting' or 'we need to have a meeting' tend to happen without focus or a clear purpose. It's like going to a sports field to play a game without specifying which game. Soccer, rugby, volleyball, basketball? Games have names that specify the rules and content to the game. Meetings need names for the same reason. Nameless meetings cause the same level of confusion and indeed exhaustion as nameless games would cause, and frequently do. The purpose, the content, the expectation resides in the allocated name.

Meetings in any organisation should really come in families – that means there should be an overall meetings structure, and sense of continuity and connection between meetings. They should not live separate lives from each other, and the agendas, tools, content and approach should reflect a commonality across the board. And as in any family they need names in order to distinguish between members.

All meetings have a second name – meeting. That really doesn't tell us very much. A stand-up morning meeting looking at the ongoing operation will have a pace and brevity different from that of a strategy meeting. A brainstorming get-together will be very different from a reporting meeting, and so on. The biggest mistake we make is not differentiating sufficiently between meeting types, and the biggest mistake of all is to have a meeting that simply does not have a name that defines its purpose and gives attendees a sense that someone has at least thought about why this meeting is happening and what its objective might be.

The organisational dead zone

No-name meetings happen all the time. They are like the orphans of the world of meetings, no one wants to own them and participants, unlike the orphans depicted in the Dickens novel *Oliver Twist*, will not be asking for more. Some teams and departments simply have meetings where everything is on the menu and the courses are not served in any discernible order. There will be a check-in, an operational update, someone will give a presentation, then coffee and cake will come out and it will devolve into random discussions and, at some point, it will stumble towards a non-conclusive ending.

Meetings cannot organise themselves, so unfortunately they show up not fully formed most of the time. They reside in what I refer to as the 'Dead Zone' of organisational life along with the results of employee satisfaction surveys, sustainability, corporate social responsibility and a myriad of other stuff. Everyone is reluctant to go there, as these topics are often seen as 11th hour inconveniences that just maybe someone might get around to when the 'serious' work is done. I have seen all kinds of strange jobs being allocated in companies – CXO this and CXO that – but I have never met anyone with the title of CEM, 'Chief Executive of Meetings'. This I find strange, surely there is some best practice to be shared, surely having a thought through approach and a highly effective meetings organiser would be priceless given the potential value of a clear and structured meetings process.

Meetings also need somewhere to live and have someone to own them. This becomes apparent when the question at the end of the meeting is "Who wants to organise the next one?" After some shiftiness in the group someone is volunteered for the job. I can promise you that person will begin the preparation for the next meeting, which if scheduled for Monday at 15.00, at about 14.47 on that day. If it's an online meeting this timescale shrinks to about 14.57. Try not to be volunteered for this duty.

Real leaders understand the importance of breathing

I once knew a company that put such a level of importance on communication that it planned its meetings in January every year. They had named meetings with differentiated agendas. These were planned and inserted in the calendar for the year in January. Then they published their meeting plan not only to managers and employees but to customers and suppliers too. Also, all invitations were sent out with time, date and location. In this case, you would need a hell of an excuse not to show up for a meeting in July when you received the invitation in January.

The message from this level of organisation is that the company knows the value of internal communication and makes it a priority. Here's the effect of that. It signifies to everyone whatever their role or profession – the marketer, engineer, accountant, or whoever – that there is a joint organisational priority that is more important than their individual efforts no matter how fantastic they may be in their specific area. That organisational priority is that they need to breathe together in a certain way at certain times and that this is non-negotiable because we want to be a fit, healthy and efficient company.

With this approach the following question always arises: "So what do I do if my main customer wants to meet and it clashes with the meeting?" Well the answer is you say, "I can't make it on that day, here are some alternatives…" There are two outcomes to this approach. The first is that it may create some short-term tension with the customer. The second is that as this policy moves forward and it becomes apparent that you have made clear commitments to managing your time and will stick to them, the world, grudgingly at first and later with great enthusiasm, starts to adapt to your timeframe.

This kind of strategy prioritises and redefines the whole messy arena of meetings in companies and it's transformational from top to bottom. It shows focus and structure and demonstrates that the company values clarity and above all its people's time. That's called leadership and it has multiple beneficial effects on motivation and productivity because it makes a priority of providing the portals through which the company can breathe. However, most leaders would see this as being something that's beneath them. They would prefer to talk strategy or pose signing an M&A agreement, despite its 30% chance of success, than spend a little time on a topic that has the potential to transform the operational capacity of their company and the motivation of employees.

The company in question here had a suite (family) of connected meetings with the entire year dotted with times, dates and downloadable agendas. Some very basic examples of how they differentiated their meetings you will find below.

1. The Operations Meeting (OPS)

These meetings exist to simply look at the current state of operations. The person in charge wants to surface any issue that may impede production in the immediate future. He will also check back to ensure that issues from the last Ops meeting have been resolved. They should have a tight agenda, be disciplined and efficient. These are usually focused, pacey and don't permit people going off on tangents. They are also usually short and happen on a daily or even more frequent basis, often standing up. The timeframe is now, and they are designed to catch small problems before they become big ones. When you attend be ready to be brief, to the point and open.

2. The Strategy Meeting (STR)

These focus on the future as well as considering how the current strategy is working. Ideally, various hypotheses will be discussed as well as potential new products or services, investments or acquisitions. These tend to happen less frequently than operational meetings. You can be creative and take some risks. What if? is the mindset to bring with you.

3. The Reporting Meeting (REP)

The emphasis here is on examining performance over a defined period. Three months is often a timeframe used. Let's say that a leader has six direct reports. They are all responsible for projects or separate parts of the business. This is a deep dive into both the operational ups and downs and the impact of the current strategy. They also serve to provide the big picture around the interdependencies between the various operational units. This is a performance reporting meeting, so the question is 'How well are you doing against your performance indicators?' in both the individual and team sense.

Each participant is reporting not just to her boss but in front of and with her colleagues. These meetings can have a tense atmosphere and some participants will feel some pressure. In one case I know the manager selects the worst performer to go first. Some people argue that this should be done on a one to one basis. I disagree and I'll explain why in the one to one section below. For you, you will need to know your performance indicators and what factors are enhancing performance and which are impeding progress. Also be ready to help colleagues.

4. One to One Meetings

South Africa won the Rugby World Cup in 2019. This was not expected given their form over the previous couple of years. Their coach, Rassie Erasmus, only took over his position in 2018 and performed a miraculous transformation. The team captain, Siya Kolisi, was interviewed following the final and was asked about the influence of Erasmus on the team. He referred to the openness Erasmus brought to team discussions. "He had no one to one meetings," he said, "everything was discussed in the team." Basically, what he was saying was that there were no secrets and no suspicion of personal deals or whatever being done with the boss. The same applies to business. The boss calling in people for one to one conversations can lead to mistrust in a team.

One to ones I think work best when they are part of the bigger whole and are focused on your personal welfare, and if your boss is so inclined, your coaching or mentoring. If they are not, then they can be awkward especially if the boss tries to cover stuff that is best discussed in a team setting. Of course, if you have real performance issues then the underlying reasons could be addressed in this forum.

Occasionally, yes, one to ones are OK but they cannot become the primary means of team management. If your boss is keen on this just be wary and say 'No thanks' if it becomes too frequent.

Meetings – and mutual team accountability

Checking back to our chapter on teams I promised to revisit the concept of mutual accountability. Your team meeting will consist of some version of the above examples. And if you are lucky your boss will have a family of meetings with names and differentiated agendas and objectives.

As a working team your leader should be able to drive mutual accountability in the team through how she runs her meetings. Remember in a properly functioning team you take some responsibility for the success of your teammates and they for yours. The team meeting is where this intangible concept can come to life, if it's run properly.

Many meetings are what I would describe as up and down affairs. That's means that the leader sits at the top of the table and participants shoot questions up to her and she delivers answers back down. This is of course a simplification but often team meetings devolve into almost a series of individual interactions with the boss as people compete for attention and focus on their individual challenges. The secret to ensuring that this doesn't happen is for the boss to change from boss to facilitator. That would mean that when Mary says, "It's really difficult to get the external contractor to deliver on time and it's holding everything up," the boss would not reply something like, "Well Mary, you really need to put more pressure on these guys or tell them we will cancel their contract." Instead she would bring Mary's problem back into the group and make it a challenge for the entire group to resolve.

I once worked with a manager who was outstanding at this. His favourite approach when such a problem arose was to ask, "Who has done this before?" and slowly he would facilitate a joint solution from the team and present it to Mary who would be totally excited by this level of support. Do this for a year and you will have a team that's buzzing. You cannot have mutual accountability unless the team does something together. This structured, public and mutually supportive way of running a meeting meets that criteria. Of course, individual accountability always exists and that's between you and your boss. Unfortunately, much organisational activity around accountability often means that after a disaster we hunt down the person we deem accountable. A very stupid, but surprisingly common interpretation.

People you will get to know at meetings

The more senior the boss who attends a meeting the weirder the behaviour of the attendees. Watch so-called 'edgy' people become lambs and observe the often surprisingly competitive positioning of some people. A well- or not so well-organised meeting usually has a point where the boss asks for input. This causes a dilemma for some people. They might have nothing to say but feel compelled to say something.

Some have great insights to offer but a fair percentage just speak to ensure they don't look totally clueless in front of the boss. Let's call this character Kurt. He is someone who can't wait to get his opinion out and he'll be jumping in at every opportunity. He will then scan the faces of those around the table for support, admiration or just to say, "look how smart I am." Try to keep a neutral countenance. If you want to say something you will need to be fast because Kurt's pleading scan of the faces has prompted Fiona to stagger out the most appalling statement possible.

"Well, I agree with Kurt, I think he made a very good point." After this you will catch them exchanging glances as Kurt's chair suddenly becomes too small to contain him and Fiona exhales and retreats into silence, her contribution made, and another meeting survived. It's not a crime to agree with someone but it's criminal when it's done in a self-serving non-value-adding way.

You will also meet Tom. He will be stern and earnest throughout. Then there is Jack from accounting who will only speak if the topic is accounting and then only reluctantly. A lot of people are afraid to have an opinion on anything outside of their own area of expertise. "Well, I wouldn't really know much about logistics," as Jack would say. You don't have to know everything about logistics to have some useful input. People like Jack, and there are lots of them, suck the oxygen out of the required exchanges by hiding in their self-made comfy silo. When things are dialling down and the boss says, "Anything else, anyone?" Tom comes into life. Just when you thought you will make the 5.30pm train Tom starts to unpick every decision. Just make sure that's not you.

Now you need to become a meeting professional

Meeting invitations will pop up on your calendar. There is a fair chance you will not be able to attend every one you are invited to. Ask for the objective of the meeting, the agenda and what contribution is expected from you. In other words, what's the name of the meeting and your reason for attending. Above all, get clarity about the timeframe. If it starts to overrun and you have a contribution try and get it in and get out of there. Try and be selective about which ones to attend. If it's just an information download then maybe you could get that information somewhere else or share attendance duties with a fellow team member.

1. Always ask permission

If you are in a meeting where five people are talking about a topic and you have a great idea, try not to jump up and grab a flip chart. Wait for the right moment and just say, "Is it OK if I just outline an idea here?" Get the nods and then do it. This is also a useful strategy for any intervention you may be making. Make people receptive before you make your move.

2. Don't be negative

You will have to listen to some drivel. Don't give it eye rolling and negative body language and comments. It adds nothing either to you as a person or a professional and in fact will detract from your impact and career. If it's that bad just make your excuses and go.

3. Get outside of your area of expertise

If you know nothing about accounting practices or manufacturing, there is no need to hide under the table when the discussion starts. You will never learn unless you are prepared to engage. Ask simple questions. People really appreciate it if you show interest and if it's the business of the team then it's your business. It's also amazing just how much you can learn and indeed win over others by making this effort.

Remember the three negative Cs

Don't complain, don't compare and don't criticise at meetings. Be straightforward and helpful. Develop a reputation for being timely, prepared and positive.

Summary

Meetings in many organisations tend to have a poor reputation for the many reasons we have looked at. They often lack focus, continuity and ownership. They need to exist in a related 'family' structure. Too often they remain nameless and pointless. Meetings should be where organisations breathe and flow. The fact that this doesn't often happen is largely due to lack of leadership attention and the lack of ownership. Therefore, the expectations of most attendees will not be high and frustrations enormous. There exists a massive opportunity to add value to your company by working on this. You really should have a go.

- Meetings are opportunities for companies to breathe. In other words, to exhale the old and inhale the new.

- No-name meetings tend to try and cover everything and lead to confusion and exhaustion.

- Meetings need names, differentiated agendas and they need to have a red line that connects the entire family.

- Mutual team accountability needs to be driven in team meetings where collaborative problem-solving is a key meeting strategy.

- One to one get-togethers with your boss are occasionally fine as long they are not the principal means she uses to manage the team.

- You will see people behave in unexpected ways in meetings. Don't be surprised, don't be impressed and don't imitate them.

CHAPTER SEVEN

Finding Meaning And Purpose At Work Of All Places

"There is no agony greater than bearing an untold story inside of you."

Maya Angelou

Organisations have tried for millennia to get groups of people to move together in the same direction whilst simultaneously defining just how members should behave towards each other at the interpersonal level. Armies are the most obvious example. Soldiers are inculcated with patriotic values and even dress codes and ways of addressing others are defined in minute detail. The military approach to this tends to be a break you down and build you up approach. In other words, they take groups of very diverse individuals and put them through extreme physical and mental challenges and through that process build strong interpersonal bonds and comradeship. Of course, all of this was and is supported by a system of extreme discipline up to and including the death penalty. But as you will see in the last chapter of this book, organisations can kill you too, they are just more subtle about it.

The most common means of getting people moving in the same direction inside companies was and indeed is the Mission, Vision and Values approach. In short, these set out to explain what the company is trying to accomplish, what its long-term perspective is, and how employees should treat each other internally and customers and suppliers externally. Whilst some companies did a reasonable job in implementing this approach, in general these statements emerged from a top management meeting to be then polished and pimped up by corporate communications and stuck on cards, websites, posters, etc.

Stuff like sustainability and corporate social responsibility got grafted on to this standard approach in recent years. All of this was printed out in copious amounts but rarely mentioned or talked about in any meaningful way. They were everywhere except in the place they were supposed to be – in the hearts and bones of every manager and every employee. In many cases they were at best wishful thinking and at worst empty promises. Remember our discussion of the values approach earlier?

In this chapter we want to explore the wider picture of change in the world and how that is influencing just how organisations try and create unity, direction, stability and meaning for their employees. For reasons we will explore in some depth here, the concept of 'purpose' is now gaining traction as the means of achieving this. This we will explore from both the individual and organisational perspectives and consider the pros and cons of this approach.

Milton's 'free lunch' turned out to be pretty expensive for a lot of people

Maybe we shouldn't be too surprised that the Mission, Vision and Values approach often appeared somewhat superficial. This is probably because at the very core of organisational existence was an economic philosophy that dictated the priorities of all executives and managers. This emanated from as far back as 1962 when the University of Chicago economist Milton Friedman could confidently state, "A company has no social responsibility to the public or society but only to its shareholders." This was epitomised in the well-known phrase 'There is no such thing as a free lunch'.

Friedman was highly influential and politicians and lawmakers drew up economic policies that favoured his approach. If you joined an organisation during that era, then the primary purpose of the organisation was simply to reward its shareholders and owners. So, as we can see, the entire Mission, Vision and Values approach as outlined above was always built on shaky ground as there was no real incentive to invest in employees and indeed society in general.

However, that started to change over the past ten years as consumers and employees began to question the practices of companies as they became more transparent. This was driven by a range of concerns including inflated executive pay, growing fiscal inequality, environmental concerns, stress at work, shareholder activism and many others, all disseminated and amplified through social media and internet-enabled instant feedback to companies. All of this caused organisations to begin to reconsider their exclusive focus on enriching shareholders and owners.

In August 2019 this all became official, if we can use that word. Almost 200 CEOs of leading American corporations got together and redefined 'the purpose of the corporation'. They issued a statement repudiating the Friedman approach and pledged a 'fundamental commitment to all of our stakeholders'. As an employee that means you too. So yes, things are changing and now the challenge is to reimagine organisations in the light of this change. What can and what should they do in order to serve this wider stakeholder constituency? To try and answer this question let's explore the external environment a bit more.

The coming of the light

Daniel Dennett, the American philosopher, likens the massive changes underway in the world and particularly in the area of digital technology, to an event from evolutionary biology. The Cambrian Explosion occurred about half a billion years ago and is marked by a sudden and extraordinary explosion in animal life on Earth.

New species appeared at a previously unseen rate. The hypothesis is that the Earth and particularly the oceans were suddenly flooded with light, forcing existing creatures to either adapt or die. Apparently, most died out and new animals with the ability to see evolved.

Dennett sees the new digital technologies, from ubiquitous camera surveillance, to facial recognition AI applications, to hacked emails, to the codification of practically all corporate and private information as eventually making privacy a thing of the past. He writes: "Every human institution from marriage to the army to the government to the courts to corporations to banks and religions, every system of civilisation is now in jeopardy because of this new transparency." The real question we are interested in is this one. Which companies will survive the coming of the light? And how might a focus on the wider stakeholder group facilitate this?

Surely, it will be the ones who have figured out that a 21st century organisation will be one that realises that authenticity and transparency will not any longer be an option, and if they cannot change then they run the risk of being wiped out by a tweet, a leaked email or a ten-second sliver of video.

The psychological state of the world

Dennett's dystopian analysis is being played out 24/7 before our very eyes. Try the following. Switch on your 24-hour, HD, blazing colour, picture-driven news channel with 3D graphics and breathless news anchors. In fact, you don't have to because it will probably find you through whatever devices you use without you even asking. You will hear of hacked emails, disrupted elections, sex tapes surfacing, the stealing of data, stolen identities, the exposure of fake PhDs, and an unending list of other stuff. I woke up in a hotel in London at 6am recently to a news headline of a crazed knifeman attacking people on a subway in Japan. I consider myself to be a pretty empathic person and of course I care, but do I need to know this before I head off to work in a city 6,000 miles from the scene of the crime?

This is not the world we used to go to work in and this is not change as we knew it. It's a world tinged with a pervasive, in-your-face firehose of negativity, fear and anxiety delivered at lightning speed to your TV, smartphone, tablet and all future versions of the above.

Professor Brené Brown, the US sociologist, brings it closer to home for all of us. She tells the following story and I paraphrase:

"I had to catch a flight that morning, on my mind was the school project my 7-year-old was struggling with and on the way to the airport I had to visit the grocery store and on the way in I see a poster about what to do in case your child gets kidnapped and as I drive on I see a sign saying that 39 people have been killed on this specific stretch of freeway and as I approached security at the airport I hear that the threat level has been raised to orange and then came the announcement about unattended baggage and then the face of my 5-year-old flashes on to my phone… it's his school calling to say he has a fever and if I can pick him up…"

She goes on to declare that Americans today are "*the most addicted, most medicated, obese and in-debt adult cohort in human history.*" What's true for the US is likely to be reflected to a large extent in other countries as well.

On the other hand, Steven Pinker from Harvard tells us that the world has never been more peaceful, prosperous or better educated and that we humans have never had it so good. All of this he supports with hard statistical evidence. The news firehose won't however be focused on the extraordinary news that Steven Pinker has to share with us, and I don't believe I have to explain why.

What about you? Where are you going to find some certainty in a world riven by uncertainty? What can companies do firstly to survive, and secondly to create a stable environment for their employees and extended stakeholder family? How will they find the authenticity and transparency which are the minimum requirements for survival in the world according to Daniel Dennett? How will they give employees a sense of belonging, inclusion and stability in both their work team and organisation at large?

Purpose has become the means to a better end

Many organisations are now turning to their immutable reason for being, that is their purpose, to provide long-term guidance and stability. This echoes the publication by the 200 CEOs on the new purpose of the organisation. The word purpose has provided the conceptual basis for many organisations looking to change today.

Again, the first challenge is what does it mean? And more specifically what does it mean to you as a person and to the organisation you are considering joining? There is nothing new about the word purpose, but it remains one of those words in common use that most of us find hard to pin down.

Professor William Damon defines purpose as follows:

"Purpose is a stable and generalised intention to accomplish something that is at the same time meaningful to the self and consequential for the world beyond the self."

This definition gives us lots to work with as we home in on gaining a more complete understanding on what purpose means for us. For those who may have thought that the word purpose was a wishy-washy, abstract, magic potion kind of concept, the notion of 'accomplishing something' as expressed above brings us right down to earth. As stated, it should be meaningful and fulfilling to the individual and be simultaneously outward looking regarding the welfare of others. So, it's only about you in so far as you can gain a sense of meaning by contributing to the world in general and those around you.

Here is the main difference between the old Mission, Vision and Values approach and the Purpose approach.

Purpose is Personal

This is a complete reversal of the old principle of having to buy into a general vision as defined by the company. This is an invitation to literally be yourself. That's a major break with the past. When organisations seek to harness individual purpose at work they are asking you to make a personal investment in yourself, your colleagues, your team and indeed the company.

If you ask a random person "What's your purpose?" the answer may well be "In what regard?" Someone in college may answer "To get a good degree." Another may say "To get a good job," whilst another may venture "To be happy." Whilst these answers may be both relevant and true at the time of asking, they come across as being time-bound general objectives or goals, rather than something that is more personal, unique and individual.

In organisational terms we look at the question of purpose from several perspectives. The unique leadership professional purpose of, for instance, individual managers or of individual contributors or indeed the (raison d'être) purpose of the organisation itself.

Exploring purpose from these perspectives poses fundamentally different questions to the ones posed above. There is no fully-formed end state to a leadership or organisational purpose, rather a continuous striving towards an ideal. You can say, "My leadership purpose is…", and you can write it down, but its realisation can only ever be its next best version of itself and its next even better version and so on. There is no full stop in the grammatical lexicon of professional purpose. It will evolve from its core over time. Walt Disney expressed this beautifully when he said, "Disneyland will never be completed as long as there is imagination left in the world."

Where does purpose come from?

Let's focus on your professional purpose irrespective of whether you are a leader or an individual contributor. If traditionally buying into the Mission, Vision and Values approach required you to consume and represent a story written by someone else, then the purpose approach demands that you write your own life story. And not only author it but accept it, own it and share it.

Our lives consist of a core set of experiences, events, ups, downs, influential figures, loves, hates, disappointments, successes, strengths, weaknesses, etc. Purpose emerges from our unique life story, in other words what's inside of you will be the content from which it's derived. It's the surfacing of this life story that's the key. We are what we have experienced, and examining, reflecting on, accepting and above all sharing our life stories are the key to understanding what unique qualities we bring to becoming a leader, team member or a great colleague. Does your purpose emerge fully formed as if you were psychologically pregnant with it, without knowing all your life? No is the answer, it doesn't. What emerges are the building blocks of memories, feelings and events along with the affirmations and confirmations of both your worth and fallibilities. It's the experience of seeking your purpose that can set you on the road to being purposeful.

Can you do this alone? Maybe, but doing it in a group using professional facilitation really tends to be the best approach. It can for instance be done in your work team or group, with storytelling being the medium and the raw material that make up your life being the content. It's astonishing to learn what others can see in you, and how they may perceive some aspect of your life in an entirely different way from the way you have carried it about for your entire life. These exchanges are not necessarily easy and revealing some of life's challenging moments in a group can be a gut-wrenching experience. This normally involves an emotional investment on the part of each participant. But if the process is easy and non-challenging and superficial then it's probably something less than real purpose you are pursuing.

Broken or broken open?

David Brooks of the *New York Times* talks of difficult life events as having two possible effects: they can 'break you' or they can 'break you open'. In other words, they can close you down and have you retreat from the rigours of living a full life. Or conversely, they can serve to open you up to accept and learn from the experience no matter how difficult it may have been. Properly conducted, a purpose discovery session can create intimacy, connection and mutual empathy at a much deeper level than you would normally experience in the workplace.

When people start sharing their life stories one of the first things you notice is just how similar the range of experiences different people have had can be. As well as creating a strong bonding effect in a group it can help the individual find affirmation, direction and balance.

The currency that's exchanged in a proper purpose conversation are authenticity, transparency and empathy. Imagine, if enough people in your organisation engage in this process then you are well on the way to being able to welcome the coming of the light as explained by Daniel Dennett, and dealing with the firestorm of negative news as outlined by Brené Brown. As a speaker, consultant and facilitator my professional purpose statement is the following:

'I make what is important interesting.'

This emerged through the process described above and is derived from my unique life story, my early life experiences, my professional experiences, my strengths, weaknesses, disappointments, successes and so on.

Some jobs may appear more purposeful than others. If you are a nurse it may appear quite easy to derive purpose and meaning from helping others and almost certainly your work will have a powerfully positive impact on your patients. But that is not a given. If you are a traffic warden, then perhaps the consensus might be that that would be more difficult. Who knows? The reality is that no job is either purposeful or not purposeful. It's you who brings purpose to whatever it is that you do. It's you who takes whatever it is you are accomplishing and imbues it with meaning. No one else can do this for you. Bosses, colleagues, organisations and the design of the task at hand can to a greater or lesser extent facilitate your success in doing this but it's you that is the key player in finding and implementing your professional purpose.

Is the boss ready for the purpose discussion?

How will your 48-year-old CXO respond when we ask him to participate in such a session? Remember he will belong to a generation of managers who got selected on their ability to configure the assets of the company in such a way that it throws out a profit, often in the shortest possible timescale. That qualification is hardly going to change. Is that skill compatible with the sensitivity and skillset needed to inculcate both people and organisation with genuine purpose? I don't see any reason why it can't be, and let's be fair, there are and always have been many, many managers and leaders who for decades have worked in a purposeful way without ever having had someone like me tell them it was a good idea. However, it can be a tough call for someone whose career has been built focusing on different priorities.

The process of the senior management team defining the purpose of the organisation initially follows the same path of the personal revelation of individual life stories in order to surface the leadership purpose of each person in the team. Having achieved this, they can address the raison d'être of the organisation they run. Questions like why, where and how the company came into existence are addressed along with its successes, missteps and future orientation.

The output from this tends to be a combination of both the rational and emotional aimed at unifying the company and influencing the daily behaviours of thousands of people. The purpose statement of Nasa reads as follows: *"To reach for new heights and reveal the unknown for the benefit of humankind."* Whether you are an astronaut or an engineer, a communications professional or an intern it applies equally to you. It takes you way beyond the job that you do to a shared feeling of togetherness in the achievement of this shared purpose. This is a giant step forward from the boiler plate Mission, Vision and Values statements of the past.

There will be people who will try and fake it

Malcolm Gladwell in his book *Blink* regaled us with the story of the Getty Museum's Greek Kouros statue in the 1980s. He focused on the immediate, spontaneous reactions of various experts who were asked to assess its authenticity. One of those was a man named Thomas Hoving who was well qualified to make an assessment. Hoving, however, had a unique way of doing this. Instead of instantly trying to apply his experience and learning in a conscious way to the task at hand, he had developed a habit of making a note of the first word that appeared in his mind on seeing a new piece of art. As he looked at the Kouros the word 'fresh' immediately came to mind. Hardly the reaction you would expect to a piece supposedly over 2,000 years old. He said to the new owner, "If you haven't already paid for it, then don't." He had listened to his gut and uncovered what he felt was a fake and a fake it proved to be.

Any given company could declare their new purpose tomorrow and run it up the flagpole for all to see. They could hang it in a 20-metre high million-dollar gold picture frame and display it in reception and every newspaper and TV station would be reporting on this amazing development. How would you know if it was the real thing? Well the first thing you should do is the Hoving trick and trust your gut reaction. If that's not enough, then ask some questions. "Where did the purpose come from, who was involved in developing it and how does the company work to sustain it?" If you get a mealy-mouthed, unclear answer, then like Mr Hoving you may well have a fake on your hands.

If your company decides to explore and embrace purpose as a means of aligning and energising the organisation then the leadership are asking their employees to make an emotional investment in their team and in the company and will have to do so themselves. This means they have a greater responsibility to ensure that their organisation knows how to communicate, steward, maintain and implement it on a long-term basis. It cannot be treated as a short-term affectation. If they do it right, they are running towards the light. If they betray it by seeing it as a fashionable and expedient branding exercise, they will deserve to end up extinct.

To do and to be – the benefits of being purposeful

1. Which list again?

We are all familiar with to-do lists. We are less so with the concept of the to-be list.

Going through the process of discovering purpose helps get you to a deeper understanding of *being* a better boss, colleague or indeed parent or friend. Having worked through the process you will get to a point where you too can write down and state your professional purpose. It's not a magic potion, but properly derived and understood it can become a powerful force for a more holistic, centred and meaningful professional and personal life.

2. The job interview

Imagine you are going for a job interview and one of the questions is "What kind of team leader will you be if you get this job?" Usually people start to talk about their strengths, successes and experience and results gained in other jobs. Imagine if you said, "Let me tell you about my professional purpose," and you did just that. Everything mentioned above would emerge from the story that you would tell, but not in a cold technical explanation, rather warmly contextualised inside of your life story and its ebbs and flows. Do this and basically what you have done is demonstrated your leadership style and approach in a considered, personal and highly resonant way.

3. Making difficult career choices

You reach a career crossroads and you have some choices to make. Having gone through the process of finding your professional purpose you will be much more in tune with your internal compass and this can inform your longer term perspective of where you would like to focus your energies and indeed lead your life.

Summary

How an organisation leads and guides its people needs to be relevant to the contemporary external environment. The world today is in a momentous state of change accelerated and sensationalised by ubiquitous media. Many people live lives riven by anxiety and the challenge for organisations is to create a stable environment for employees. As the philosophy underlying the economic existence of companies morphs into something more responsible and caring, the opportunity arises to reimagine organisations that provide a greater sense of belonging, transparency and authenticity. The concept of purpose in its different forms has emerged as the vehicle to accomplish this.

- There has been a seismic shift in the existential underpinnings of organisations with stakeholder value replacing shareholder value as a key principle.

- Social and traditional media threaten to swamp us with non-stop anxiety-inducing 'news' from a world changing at a rate of knots previously unseen.

- Organisations have a duty to realise and engage with the new stakeholder focus thus bringing a fresh impetus to the company/employee relationship.

- Getting to a real sense of purpose is messy, challenging and emotional. It's usually far better to do it in a group setting where you will benefit from the reflections of others and you can also play that role in helping them.

- Your purpose can serve you well as a means of staying centred, making decisions and living more holistically both in business and in life.

- It can be of great practical use in presenting yourself to others, in many different situations, such as a job interview or introducing yourself to a new group.

CHAPTER EIGHT

Purpose And Agile: An Organisational Marriage Made In Heaven?

"The neglected leadership role is the designer of the ship."

Peter Senge

When Christopher met Isabella

When Christopher Columbus was in startup mode and getting his first round of finance together he wasn't getting much traction around his hometown of Genoa. So, he gets himself to Spain and talks the Queen into backing his new venture. This was in short to try and connect Europe to Asia by a sea route. We all know what happened and why we ended up calling native Americans Indians. On his first voyage he was away for about eight months. We are unsure if the Queen had concerns about the potential success of her investment, but in any case, she couldn't get him on WhatsApp or call him on his mobile or check in on Slack to see how the team was doing. He was out of sight. When he finally got back, I can only suppose that the only question the Queen could ask him was, "Well, how did it go?" Not bad at all would have been his answer before they got into the second round of funding discussion.

Imagine your boss only having the possibility of asking "how did it go?" when you finish your first big project. There are only two possibilities to ensure this occurs. Either your boss is very cool and is aware that you have what it takes to work with minimal supervision, or you are both working in a structure or space that enables this behaviour and makes it the norm.

Intuitively we imagine that the history of leadership in the 21st century must be one of the gradual broadening of the decision-making function to a wider group. Steven Denning talks of not moving decisions up a corporate hierarchy, but of 'moving the competence down to where the best-qualified people can make them'. It's a brilliantly articulated idea but the world of business has never been less equipped to accommodate this. Every boss has the means to be in contact with every direct report in real time. Every subordinate knows this. If I know that my boss is simply a text message away, then why should I make this tricky decision alone? After all, if it goes wrong there could be consequences. From the boss's perspective, checking in is a massive temptation. When I discussed this recently with a manager he said, "I do check in a lot with my direct reports and they with me. My boss checks with me a lot so I need to have details for her. We are getting the results, so why change it?"

How did it go?

Whatever happened to Queen Isabella's "How did it go?" after Columbus had been away for eight months spending her money? We can conclude two things from all of this. Firstly, that despite the advent of words like empowerment and the established knowledge we possess over the beneficial effects of autonomy and self-directed teams, those in charge still find it difficult to resist controlling and influencing their subordinates. And now they have the electronic tools to do it all day, every day if they wish.

Secondly, if a situation exists where it's simply not possible for the boss to permanently check in and harass direct reports then maybe we have the potential to recreate the structure and conditions like those which prompted the Queen of Spain to ask Columbus her question. In other words, we need to create an ocean of space between the manager and the subordinate and do that by creating a structure that largely dispenses with the role of close supervision as a leadership task.

In this chapter I want to get you thinking more broadly about the organisational structures. And, I will endeavour to assist you in figuring out just how far the company you may be entering has progressed in its thinking regarding its structure and how well that structure facilitates more freedom for you to get your work done. We will also look at the combination of structure and the complementary leadership prerequisites necessary to optimise the outcomes. Finally, I will request that you consider just how well can you live with ambiguity, uncertainty, speed and decision making. Don't forget that less direct supervision will mean more responsibility for you.

The original point of organisational structure

Early factories, particularly in the automotive industry, had gantries overlooking the factory floor. This gave management the opportunity to 'oversee' the workers as they went about their tasks. Office architecture over the past century has stayed true to this idea of vertical separation with those above looking down on those below. The executive suite tends not to be on the first floor.

The same notion applies if we think of it in terms of an organisational chart which looks like a pyramid built from boxes with a decreasing number of boxes as you ascend until you get to the one at the top. This structure designates roles and responsibilities, it defines boundaries and allocates power to individuals and assigns decision-making responsibilities according to the 'level' of the person in the system. Big decisions are taken at the top, smaller ones, hopefully, at the bottom and there's a need for a lot of coordination up and down the system, making it slow and cumbersome.

This structure has been around a long time and characterises most large human groupings from political parties to the church to the military and even to criminal gangs. Business did not invent it, but it was adopted by most companies worldwide and the majority still work in some form of this model. The point of this organisational structure was control. This focus on control assumed that most people in the organisation could not be trusted to make decisions. It's under great pressure today and we see that in the problems experienced by hierarchical institutions of all kinds. It's difficult to maintain control when the people you seek to control are too well educated and independent and have the same access to information and indeed to the press and other channels of publicity as those in charge.

It was built for different people in a different time. It was built when there was a strict demarcation between thinking and doing. People at the top thought and the people at the bottom did. However, there is at least one valuable lesson we can take from this organisational structure. History shows that some managers have made it work extremely well. How can that be possible? Well, the lesson we need to learn is that great leadership, i.e. leadership that values and consults its people, encourages decision making at every level, maintains a sense of humility, and optimism can break out of even the most outmoded cage it finds itself in. Imagine the possibilities when great leadership is facilitated rather than restricted by the structure it finds itself in.

To think or to do

A statement from Frederick Taylor, the leading management thinker of the early 20th century, reflects that old thinking versus doing mindset: '*One of the very first requirements for a man who is fit to handle pig iron as a regular occupation is that he shall be so stupid and so phlegmatic that he more nearly resembles in his mental make-up the ox than any other type.*'

Taylor was a pioneer in the organisation of work, and indeed most organisations functioning today will have been influenced by his work in some shape or form. He was simply stating that in his theory of organisation and at that time, the division of labour was a key facet in gaining optimal productivity. In hindsight maybe he could have expressed himself differently, but these were very different times.

Whilst things did improve throughout the 20th century the vertical hierarchy continued to be the form of choice for most companies and often they resembled vast bureaucratic pyramids. You had to know your place. What was it like to be an employee in such a hierarchy? One observer wrote: 'People leave their office window open so that their souls can escape.' This neatly encapsulates the feeling of restriction and powerlessness the sheer weight of hierarchy can bring to bear on an individual.

These days everyone is expected to think – maybe not everyone about a great acquisition target, but certainly about helping customers solve problems. People are better educated, attitudes have changed, and they simply don't need the command and control style of leadership inherent in such a system. They have many more choices regarding possible occupations and making tangible objects, which most people did when hierarchies were introduced is no longer the only or primary function of companies. Machines increasingly do more and more of the hands-on work today. Completely new industries have arisen that don't make anything solid and certainly don't fit into the old organisational model. New businesses and entire new industries abound. Technology has speeded up processes, customers demand instant service. Something had to change in organisational design, and it did.

The new point of organisational structure

Research by Stanford Professor Gary Hamel demonstrates that the result of over a century of having lived and worked in this structure on a worldwide basis means that the average ratio of manager to employee is an astonishing 1 to 4.7 or as he puts it "one bureaucrat for every 4.7 employees." He estimates that people are spending about one day per week on internal bureaucratic tasks and in many organisations much more. These ratios will differ across industry segments and indeed countries, but the message is clear, that the legacy of hierarchy is a lack of autonomy.

Hamel uses the example of a GE factory in North Carolina where one person supervises 400 workers. This prompts the question of who makes the decisions in this factory and we can safely assume that they have a structure that ensures decisions are made inside of a format where the employees feel empowered to do so. Somehow the power previously locked up in the organisational chart has been transferred to these employees. Hamel goes on to look at the possible economic effects of major structural change. "What would happen if you put the non-productive bureaucratic work back into the economy in a more productive way?" he asks. He estimates that it would have a greater economic impact than any public policy proposal or technology implementation available today.

It's not just that the forms organisations take will influence employee motivation, productivity and service, but cumulative change across industry could be a vehicle for massive economic progress simply though shifting the organisational shape and the leadership prerequisites to go with it. The inflexibility of the old way drove organisations to seek alternative models. And of course, it was out of one of these new industries that a new and competing structural model emerged. Necessity was, in this case, the mother of invention. Before we look at this alternative model let's just dive a bit deeper into the possibilities of releasing the engagement, energy and productivity inherent in people that the old controlling hierarchical model largely got in the way of.

The hunt for the Holy Grail

Daniel Pink, the researcher and writer, highlights three basic concepts underlying successful workplaces. These he has termed Autonomy, Mastery and Purpose. Roughly they translate as freedom from close controls, i.e. employees are trusted to get on with their work. Secondly, what he terms mastery, the human desire to improve and use their strengths. And finally purpose with its sense of meaning and fulfilment a person may derive from their work.

As an example of autonomy in action he explains a practice initiated by the Australian software company Atlassian. They give their developers periods of time when they can work on whatever project they want to with whoever they want and it's during these times of extraordinary autonomy they find that the most outstanding work gets done.

It's not that Pink has dug up a treasure that no one else knew existed. Try reading employee surveys or talking to people at work and you get the same complaints. 'My boss won't let me get on with stuff, I'm just a cog in the wheel and I never see the results of my work,' are complaints that are frequently heard. When it comes to employees using their strengths, Gallup reports that less than 30% of all workers worldwide report that they get to use their strengths every day.

In 1959 Frederick Herzberg presented his famous two factor theory of motivation where he concluded that decent working conditions, for instance a fair salary, paid holiday time, various fringe benefits etc., were in themselves insufficient to increase employee motivation. These were necessary to keep employees 'satisfied' but insufficient to motivate them to higher levels of performance. He went on to identify motivational factors that were inherent or intrinsic to the work itself. These he identified as challenge, responsibility, growth opportunities and recognition. Pink's work largely overlaps with these findings. Considering the personal psychological needs and motivations of the individual worker was revolutionary thinking at the time. However, to this day, employers still invest heavily in 'working conditions' and wonder why motivation and productivity does not rise accordingly. There are other, more important factors at play.

Intrinsic and extrinsic motivation

A former English Premier Football League manager knows something about motivation. He had a unique way of accessing the intrinsic motivation of young footballers. These 20-year-olds earned vast sums of money and, as we know, that would not be enough to ensure motivation to ever higher performance and team success. When asked about this and how he deals with it he explained, "I get them together at the start of the season and we get together and talk and I ask them to recall their boyhood days when they started to play football. And they will tell stories about the school team, and the under 14 league and all that experience in the mud and rain with parents and siblings watching and so on. And when I ask them how it felt as a boy they will say things like fantastic, amazing and when they get to that point of reflection I say to them, 'That's who I want playing for me, that boy you still are in your heart with all the pride and emotion of playing football for the sheer joy of it'." He clearly understood the potential of intrinsic motivation.

All of us are motivated by an internal desire to behave in a certain way because we find it satisfying and fulfilling in and of itself. For instance, many countries offer incentives to the public for the donation of blood and plasma. In some countries the main strategy tends to be not to offer financial rewards but simply to let people feel the internal satisfaction of performing this good and important civic deed. In fact, in New Zealand studies have shown that the offer of such rewards can deter potential donors.

Earlier this century Microsoft's Encarta, an online information resource from a vast commercial company, succumbed to Wikipedia which was developed and run by people for no salary whatsoever. There are many such examples.

The forces that have pushed us towards a new and more flexible organisation were many and varied. Market demands for speed and innovation; new industries needing a new approach; better educated and more independent workers; research and experience clearly showing the sheer power of autonomy and motivation when nurtured and engaged at work. The leadership challenge then is finding a way to engage the strengths and the infinite intrinsic motivations of people at work, and one prerequisite for that is a structure and a system that is flexible, responsive, empowering and self-directing.

A purpose-made organisation

Let's imagine for a moment that a company has fully embraced the tenets of purpose as discussed in the previous chapter at both the individual and organisational level. The management and many employees would have experienced the intense shared process of discovering their individual purpose. Career plans would have been changed, leadership styles altered, and new and powerful relationships forged. They would have found a greater sense of meaning and fulfilment in their work and be energised to meet the challenges that come their way with a greater sense of mutual trust and commitment. The senior team, and ideally others from throughout the company, would have additionally questioned and debated and reoriented the raison d'être of the company given the realities of the world outside and the zeitgeist of the times.

Let's take our imagining one step further. If you then took that group of people and asked them to design an organisational structure that would optimally facilitate the emergent mindset of the management and employees, what would that look like? Would they design a hierarchy with power locked away in a hierarchical pyramid? Well, probably not. The key words on their drawing board would probably be meaning, autonomy, strengths, collaboration and flexibility. Looking at the world outside they would add transparency, speed and responsiveness. What would our managers and employees say if they were asked to return to the stodgy old hierarchical organisation? What would they do if they were told to go and design their own organisational structure? We can't say exactly but just maybe it exists in some form already.

Agile – an idea has come of age

Companies are increasingly adopting the agile structure. Agile means 'able to move quickly and easily', which is much better than the slowness and stiffness of the old model. This structure emerged from an industry that simply did not exist when the old-style hierarchical pyramid was conceived. That's the software industry. Having spent years trying to retrofit this new industry into the old hierarchical box, developers gave up and decided they had to reinvent the space in which they wanted to work. Trying to meet customer demands in developing software inside of a hierarchical structure was frustrating.

Unlike the development of a classic solid industrial product, customer expectations around software were that it could be done more quickly and that changes could be made on the fly right up to the delivery date. This caused enormous frustration among software developers. Thus was born the Agile movement which has in the meantime become an all-encompassing organisational structure across practically every business segment including the heavier engineering and product companies.

Interestingly, the work 'movement' often appears in the agile world and it's still seen to be somewhat revolutionary as it is so drastically different in approach from the traditional structure.

Here is an extract from the original agile manifesto:

Individuals and interactions over processes and tools.

Working software over comprehensive documentation.

Customer collaboration over contract negotiation.

Responding to change over following a plan.

That is, while there is value in the items on the right,

we value the items on the left more.

This was very innovative thinking at the time, which was prompted by a genuine need, so it found immediate traction. Most importantly it came directly from people in the field working every day to find new ways to deliver a better product more quickly to their customers. Whilst it began in the new world of software development it spread quickly to other industries. For example, the US company John Deere who produce machinery for a range of business areas including agriculture and construction was an early adopter. They had great success improving innovation project times by up to as much as 75% using agile. In addition, team engagement ratings improved significantly and quality showed marked gains. Finally, an optional structure was available and an increasing number of companies are betting on it.

Agile in action

Whilst the central tenets of agile are universal, many different flavours of the approach have evolved. It is first and foremost action oriented. It is immediate in so far that information is shared in a defined and ritualised manner and information is made visible to all on a recurring basis. Agile is customisable and whilst all versions are based on the same principles, they can look somewhat different according to the nature of the business and individual company priorities. Companies will also use different nomenclature to describe the various moving parts. Below I give a short description of one standard approach.

Employees are not grouped by departments but by disciplines. These groupings are called chapters. So, if you are an IT specialist you would belong to the IT chapter. There could be an engineering chapter, a HR chapter, marketing chapter and so on. The work units are called squads. These are small, about six members, *autonomous teams* that take on a project from start to finish. They work with and close to the customer and have full visibility of what they are delivering. One team member is designated as product owner and determines exactly what they are working on, the backlog of work to be done and the to-do priority list.

But this person is not the boss. The duties of the traditional departmental boss in this setup are covered by the chapter leads to which each team member will belong. The day to day support to overcome blockages or disagreements are the responsibility of someone termed an agile coach. When the project is completed the participants will be reassigned to new squads. The largest holding groups are called tribes. These comprise a collection of squads who are working on projects that have some connection to each other. The tribe leader ensures that coordination takes place, budgets are allocated and resources are shared across the squads.

Let's imagine that you have joined a company that has adopted the agile form. In this example you will be assigned to a project squad. When you arrive at work you will attend a stand-up meeting every morning. Standing, instead of being slumped in a seat, saves time and adds a sense of urgency and action to proceedings. These meetings are aimed at clarifying progress to all team members by the team members themselves. Not by a boss who traditionally chaired such a meeting (the chair is no longer there).

Basically, each team member is required to answer three questions:

- What she did yesterday

- What she is doing today

- What impediments may be standing in the way of getting the work done

These interactions are supported by a simple set of tools that make everything visible and permits the team to track progress. These include product backlogs – what's to be done – as well as burndown charts to show progress as work gets completed. These meetings surface any problems immediately not giving them a chance to fester and drive real collaboration as the focus is on the progress of the complete team. This means that it's not possible for one individual to forge ahead alone, or indeed get left behind. Full disclosure in real time creates real energy and team ownership of solutions drives fast and immediate collaboration.

Is purpose the corporate soulmate of agile?

After 1,000 years of hierarchy it's not a given that every person and every organisation can adapt to this and it's proving to be a slow process. Structures are relatively easy to change, and offices can be redesigned and vertical structures can be flattened. That's about 10% of the challenge. The other 90% is what is commonly referred to as mindset. Can people adapt to the freedom, the openness, the independence and even the speed required to ensure that the agile organisation will deliver on its great promise? More importantly can leaders understand and embrace a job that for many will mean switching from being wielders of power to releasers of the power in others?

If we recall the key words on the drawing board for the group we commissioned to design the purpose-made organisation, they were meaning, autonomy, strengths, collaboration and flexibility as well as transparency, speed and responsiveness. If we ask the question 'how well does an agile shape facilitate these?' we would have to answer a great deal better than the previous model. But of course, it's not as easy as that. If the demands of control will prove lesser, then greater freedom and greater responsibility do not come without a price tag. Working faster and closer to the customer will test your tolerance for decision making in an ambiguous and changing world.

Purpose, as we learned, granted each person a sense of personal freedom to discover their own professional purpose. Through that process strong bonds will have built between team members and our experience tells us that on squad formation, teams tend to revisit and share that powerful experience.

The points of contact between the purpose mindset and the agile structure are undoubtedly complementary and organisations with great leadership and a strong sense of purpose will surely thrive by bringing these two facets of organisational life together. So when you get the question "How did it go?" from your boss whom you haven't seen for months because she was busy on future strategies and new markets you can surely answer in the affirmative.

Summary

The structure you work in can really affect the quality of communications and indeed leadership style in an organisation. A changing world has ensured that structures are changing from those built to control employees to those designed to liberate ideas and promote more autonomy. This can be incredibly powerful when given the room to grow and expand inside of a suitable structure, and most importantly with the right leadership. The biggest challenge to achieving this is adjusting the meaning and practice of leadership and supervision. Agile is now becoming the organisational structure of choice for many companies. Combined with purpose it holds great promise.

- Organisations were designed in order to control the activities of employees and ensure compliance with rules and regulations.

- As new industries developed, and companies discovered that offering their employees more autonomy and freedom brought greater success, looser and less restraining structures developed. Agile is the predominant example of such a structure.

- If you interview with a company who is adopting agile or already has done so then go for it. It demonstrates that the management have thought about change in a serious way. If it's a new industry then so much the better; if it's an older company in the adjustment phase then watch out, but it could still be a great learning opportunity.

- As an employee the agile world really puts you up front. Silence won't be an option in your agile team. Communication, influence and confidence will be key areas of development.

- Decisions will need to be made often without the benefit of reams of data. Speed is important. Working in an ambiguous world can be demanding and requires the ability to develop comfort in ambiguity.

- If your company sees agile as simply a different shaped box that's meant to do wonders, beware. It works best when accompanied by an effort to change the ways of leading and collaborating. The process of purpose is the best way we have seen so far to achieve that.

CHAPTER NINE

Staying Healthy, Wealthy And Wise At Work

"According to the Mayo Clinic, the person you report to at work is more important for your health than your family doctor."

Bob Chapman, CEO, Barry Wehmiller

When I was a teenager music was sold on vinyl discs. Every week radio stations counted the number sold and proclaimed a Number 1 best-selling record. There was a wide selection from Glam Rock to Disco, Punk to Metal to Hard Rock. There was less choice than today, but you did get your hands on a piece of solid vinyl and people of that era have strong memories of that experience.

Anyway, years later I became an executive coach. One of the key tasks when working with groups is getting them to open up and talk about themselves as a means of getting people acquainted with each other on more than merely a professional level. I would sometimes pose the following question to individuals: "What was your favourite music back then when you were a teenager?" I remember one group where a man in a grey suit who on answering seemed to forget himself and became animated as he told us he was a punk rocker who wore a pin in his nose, torn T-shirts and ripped jeans. He also explained that the Sex Pistols were his favourite group and that *Anarchy in the UK* was his favourite record. Then as he seemed to get embarrassed by his own spontaneous candidness, he became coy and slunk back into his grey business persona, not to resurface for the rest of the event.

I was left wondering what had happened to that young kid full of energy, life and rebellion. What had happened to the spark I witnessed when he recalled that time? Work had happened to him. That was the answer. Work had come and transformed him into someone less colourful, less optimistic and less himself. The recurring question in my head when I work and talk with today's generation is 'Will we change you boys and girls into a bunch of grey suits, or will you change us and our organisations into something much, much better?'

Electronic empathy

For much of the last eight chapters I have been attempting to sensitise you to the potential pitfalls inherent in organisational life. Let's now take that one step further and look at the implications of poor leadership, poorly managed change and overwork on your wellbeing.

We live in an age where empathy has become trivialised and commoditised, where condolences are transmitted electronically without ever having to originate anywhere near the heart of the sender. 'Thoughts and prayers' are the stock in trade of politicians and other public figures when disaster strikes, sounding more like a public duty than a genuine expression of remorse. As discussed earlier in this book, given the aspects of the non-stop bad news we endure through all the devices we carry we should be careful not to become inured to the feelings of distress and unhappiness in others. And yes, switching off and reducing exposure is an option.

Organisations are above all social structures consisting of human beings. People under pressure in organisations can be hyper-competitive, unfair, downright dishonest, bullying, nasty and aggressive. When people are put under pressure and they feel that their very livelihood is at stake these very worst elements of human behaviour can come into play. Resilience training is the escape hatch for organisations that don't know how to deal with poor leadership or help resolve workplace conflicts.

People are told to develop thicker skins and many simply end up adopting a passive-defensive stance characterised by statements like 'I'm fine and I'm just going to get on with my stuff and I'm just not getting involved'. So they don their suit of armour and their focus switches to self-protection rather than teamwork or productivity. It's the most valuable employees, i.e. those who are most engaged and committed, who refuse to disengage, who get damaged the most in a situation where conflicts are not resolved.

In this chapter we will explore work from the perspective of wellbeing and sanity. Let me say clearly that I am not a health professional, so I'll simply be sharing my own experiences, thoughts and ideas with you here.

Health – safety and pain

All organisations have an emphasis on health and safety these days and that's to the credit of the people who pushed for this over the years and to the professionals who take care of us today. Safety does take precedence over health. A broken leg or physical injuries are immediate and tangible and quite naturally need to be dealt with as a matter of urgency. In most countries there is clear legislation about how, at least, physical work should be carried out and great investment in both training and equipment to ensure the safety of employees. This has improved exponentially over the last decade or so.

Stress and mental health issues are less salient, and people may be very reluctant to discuss them, but this doesn't make them any less important. But there is undoubtedly a gap in emphasis between physical and mental health in the workplace. The work of Naomi Eisenberger, the American social psychologist, could help bridge this gap. She was fascinated that people's description of emotional hurt were often described in the same terms that people use to describe physical pain. 'My heart was broken', 'It was like a slap in the face', or 'I felt crushed', to give some examples of what people say when emotionally wounded.

You will often hear these admonitions as people describe negative work experiences.

In the workplace emotional bruising often comes in the shape of rejection and marginalisation. The feeling of a 'slap in the face' was only last week related to me by an employee as he talked about the lack of support he received from his boss when he felt rejected and sidelined by the team he belonged to. He was shaken and upset. Eisenberger was curious enough to do some neurological research into the effects of rejection. Monitoring brain activity on human rejection she found that 'being socially rejected triggered the same neural circuits that process physical injury'. In other words, 'the brain makes no distinction between broken bones and a broken heart'. As she put it, 'the pain is not just in the head, it's in the head because it's in the brain'. An astonishing and disturbing conclusion.

Inflicting deliberate physical injury on a colleague at work is a rare and obviously criminal event. Yet conflicts and inappropriate behaviour such as bullying, exclusion and cheating on colleagues at work is not uncommon and is a source of great stress for many.

The figure below is not based on any scientific research. It simply represents and summarises my own impressions of having listened to both official and particularly unofficial personnel evaluations over the years. The continuum between the two points below is probably the most common area of focus I have heard when individuals are discussed in terms of performance or promotion.

TOUGH■■■■■■■■■■■■■■■■■■■■■■■■■■■■■■■■■■■■■■■WEAK

It does offer a window into the mindset of people in organisations with the underlying assumption that a type of Darwinian selection process is acceptable and if you can't deal with it then maybe all your other great attributes are simply not worthy of consideration. This kind of attitude simply acknowledges and accepts the negative aspects of a workplace and suppresses any hope for change.

Let me give you a few more facts about the seriousness of workplace stress. Jeffrey Pfeffer reports that between 2008 and 2010 about 46 employees committed suicide at France Telecom with observers blaming cost cutting and reorganisations. A young intern at a City bank in London collapsed and died after working 72 hours straight, the coroner's report stating that he died from an epileptic fit likely brought on by stress and fatigue.

We cannot have a pain-free life and none of us will, that's a given. There will always be an element of healthy competition and personality clashes in the workplace, and that's even necessary to produce the sparks of innovation and progress. We cannot sanitise working relationships, nor should we try. But all of us know the difference between healthy debates and bullying, collaboration and exploitation, honesty and cheating and so on. We must in every sense as individuals and organisations do much, much better.

What's your number?

I remember my first pay packet. In those days you got cash in an envelope. It was a great feeling of accomplishment and independence. Money and all types of reward are important, and as you begin to earn money, I urge you to enjoy the feelings of being rewarded for the contribution you are making. Of course, money has somehow managed to get a bad reputation and we all know why. It's an extrinsic motivator with a wonderful PR operation after all, so some caution might be in order.

The American Psychological Association (APA) in 2015 reported that the two main causes of stress are work and money. This is ironic as I can imagine that money is the main reason that people stay in stressful workplaces. I have heard the maxim 'Yeah, it's tough but I'd never get the same money anywhere else' a thousand times. I wonder how it applies to Wall Street bankers.

In Wall Street financial circles there is a question often asked. It's "What's your number?" The question allegedly refers to the amount of money a person would like to accumulate in order to be able to stop working on Wall Street and go away and start, I assume, living what they would see as a worthwhile life. In the film *Wall Street: Money Never Sleeps* when the character played by Shia Le Boeuf asks the character played by Josh Brolin this question, the answer he gets is 'more'. Obviously, he hadn't yet quite worked out what a worthwhile life looked like.

This is a case of people going to work in order to create the possibility of not having to go to work. It stands to reason that they consider their current occupation either too stressful or even too immoral to be part of a life they would regard as good and reputable. So, in a convoluted way, the APA report is spot on for Wall Street as well. If the 'number' story is true, then here are people postponing 'life' in order to accumulate money in a job they clearly do not hold in any regard so that they can eventually find a job or a life they can cherish. Not sure I would want to do that, what about you?

Money does little for our happiness. Most ultra-rich people recognise this. Bill Gates is leaving nearly all his fortune to charity. He has said of his children, "They are never going to be poorly off. Our kids will receive a great education and some money, but they'll go out and have their own careers. It's not a favour to kids to have them have huge sums of wealth. It distorts anything they might do." Gates today dedicates his life and his fortune to eradicating diseases such as polio in the world through his charitable foundation. He has never looked happier or more contented. At some point in your life you too will be compelled to define what real wealth means to you and the sooner you do this the better.

Meaning, accomplishment and purpose never dies

Studs Terkel, the American author and oral historian, published a book called *Working* in 1974. This was at a time before attitudes to work became buried under mounds of employee surveys and the avalanche of books, from leadership to career management to mindfulness from amazon.com and elsewhere. Terkel was interested in the experience of ordinary men and women as they went through their working lives and he met them face to face. Terkel sensed in his subjects 'more than a slight ache' about the longing for a day's work to provide more than a pay cheque to provide a measure of meaning.

A Brooklyn firefighter named Tom Patrick goes to the heart of the matter: 'The quest for worth in a world of bad news, abstract accomplishments and intangible goals':

"The f***in' world's so f****ed up, the country's f****ed up. But the firemen, you see them produce. You see them put out a fire. You see them come out with babies in their hands. You see them give mouth-to-mouth when a guy's dying. You can't get around that sh*t. That's real. To me, that's what I want to be. I worked in a bank. You know, it's just paper. It's not real. Nine to five and it's shit. You're lookin' at numbers. But I can look back and say I helped put out a fire. I helped save somebody. It shows something I did on this earth."

This account is remarkably like other research done in the intervening years. Meaning and self-worth, purpose and a visible outcome. One wind turbine manufacturer I worked with handled the visibility part very well. They realised that not all their employees involved in the production of these massive and complex machines had the opportunity to see and experience the final product. They organised visits to wind farms in a programme they called 'Touch the Turbine' to give their office workers exactly that opportunity. This was a brilliant recognition of a need that so often goes unmet.

Terkel summarised wonderfully when he wrote that *Working* was '*about a search for daily meaning as well as daily bread, for recognition as well as cash, for astonishment rather than torpor; in short for a sort of life rather than a Monday through Friday sort of dying*'. Print this up and hang it in the office and when you go for an interview and they ask you for your expectations of working at the company, pull it out and read it to them and listen to what they have to say.

Remind me again, is stress good or bad for you?

The world is full of theories about stress. Is it good for you or is it bad for you? Is some good and some bad? Maybe it's your attitude that counts. Maybe a tough childhood would have made you less susceptible. Think about it, it's a confusing landscape. There is only one real differentiating factor at work that I want you to understand regarding stress and that's the concept of control.

Imagine you are in the car driving through a strange city and your partner is sitting next to you and you have GPS satnav running as well. You have a baby and a three-year-old in the back. It's raining and you are at a complex junction unsure whether to go straight on or turn right immediately or 50 metres further on. The GPS satnav is rerouting and your partner is loudly insisting that you turn right. You think straight on is best. There are motorcycles driving at speed between the lines of cars, and the baby has started to cry, and your blood pressure is skyrocketing. You have the dreadful feeling of not being in control. It's an unpleasant experience, accompanied by shortness of breath, a racing heart and slight nausea. You may well shout at your partner to shut the hell up and see to the baby.

Imagine you are at work and as the only breadwinner in your house you have, metaphorically speaking, your entire family with you. Your boss continually changes her mind regarding a task you are working on and you are feeling unable to proceed, but you are aware that the product manager in your neighbouring department is waiting on you to finish. Again, you have the awful feeling of not being in control of your own fate.

Control means that you have a strong say in what you are expected to deliver, when it should be delivered and to what quality standard. In other words, you have a measure of control over the outcomes of your own work. If at work your sense of control is being continually taken away and you want to shout out in protest, you can't because this is work. So, you sigh and supress your feelings and if you do that often enough over an extended period then you are setting yourself up for stress-related illness.

Work is a place where people earn their daily bread. For many the pressing need to survive in an increasingly inequitable world makes any threat to that extremely debilitating. If even your best efforts are continually monitored and changed or dismissed by someone else, it produces a helplessness and emptiness that can completely undermine your confidence. If your very best is not good enough then you feel you have literally lost the skills that you possess in your hands or the practised abilities in your head and the commitment in your heart. You feel as if you are being stripped of the very thing that brings you to work. You are not worth your desk-space, your computer, your phone, much less your salary. You almost become an imposter in your own professional life. A dangerous situation to your health and wellbeing.

Fun, optimism and regret

At a Ford car manufacturing plant in the US in November 1940 a worker named John Gallo was fired after being 'caught in the act of smiling' and 'slowing down the line for maybe half a minute'. I was once told off for organising football on the lunch break for a group of very bored industrial trainees. I also witnessed a young intern being pulled up for singing too close to the executive offices. Yes, singing.

Does work have to be fun? Well, not all of it, but for sure some of it. Humour is a classic stress reliever, without some semblance of it in the workplace tension and stress will dominate. When humour disappears from a group of people engaged on a challenging task then you can be sure that it will be replaced by stress and withdrawal.

Another way to think even more long term is the concept of regret. 'I don't have any regrets' is a common refrain from those we often perceive to be self-confident people. This probably in all honesty says more about fear than self-confidence. It reveals a lack of self-awareness and an inability to reflect and take ownership of our own missteps. It's a bit like saying I have never had to apologise for anything. Everyone has regrets because everyone has made mistakes and indeed mistakes that hurt others. Everyone has said or done something worthy of apology in their life and not to face these facts is dangerous. Susie Steiner in *The Guardian* summarises research made into the regrets expressed by those who are close to death:

1. I wish I'd had the courage to live a life true to myself, not the life others expected of me.

2. I wish I hadn't worked so hard.

3. I wish I'd had the courage to express my feelings.

4. I wish I had stayed in touch with my friends.

5. I wish that I had let myself be happier.

Nope, no mention of cash here. Steve Jobs concluded his 2005 commencement speech at Stanford University with the advice, "Stay hungry, stay foolish." The hungry will keep you moving and the foolish will keep you sane.

Summary

Work has the funny habit of winning every argument. 'Sorry, I have to go to work', 'I'll be late for work', 'I can't make it, I have to go to work'. We hear these refrains time and again. For generations we have predicted that the young people coming into work were going to change everything. Some things have changed but not as quickly or as comprehensively as many imagined. So be aware of who you are becoming as the pressure inherent in today's workplace starts to try and squeeze you into something you are not. Your health is more important than your wealth and your worth is inside of you, not in your role, title, corner office or car. Above all, enjoy work and stay optimistic. Be kind and decent, that's what people will remember. You will make stupid decisions and will have regrets. Reflect, accept and move on.

- Work can transform you into someone you fundamentally are not. It can absorb your energy, time and personality in such a way that you may not even notice until it's too late.

- Feelings of empathy and compassion are too often substituted by cut and paste text and are relegated to the 'done box'.

- Safety comes before health in most workplaces and that's understandable and has proved effective. Companies are now addressing stress, bullying and mental health at an ever-increasing rate.

- Money is wonderful and always be grateful for the opportunity to earn a decent income. When it becomes an obsession or the main priority of your time at work, you may end up serving it rather than having it serving you.

- Intrinsic motivation, meaning and the opportunity to excel at something are the proven drivers of success and enjoyment at work.

- Some measure of control over what you do and what you produce is at the centre of avoiding workplace stress and associated illnesses.

References

Adkins, Amy - Gallup
Majority of US Employees Not Engaged Despite Gains in 2014
28 January 2015

Altucher, James
https://jamesaltucher.com/blog/how-to-say-yes/

Board Agenda & Mazars
Board Leadership in Corporate Culture: European Report
Research Report in association with INSEAD
2017

Brison, Todd
Fired for smiling?
Medium.com
10 January 2018

Brooks, David
The Moral Peril of Meritocracy
Our individualistic culture inflames the ego and numbs the spirit
Failure teaches us who we are
6 April 2019

Brown, Professor Brené
The Price of Invulnerability
at TEDxKC
12 October 2010

Carlzon, Jan
Moments of Truth
Harper Business: Reprint edition
15 February 1989

Chamorro-Premuzic, Tomas
Three Reasons You Aren't Reaching Your Full Potential
Fast Company
12 July 2015

Chowdary, Dr Nagendra V
Consulting Editor, Effective Executive and Associate Dean
Icfai Business School Case Development Centre,
Hyderabad
Interview with Professor Michel Beer
June 2007

Churchwell, Sarah
If you want to run the world study a 'useless' subject
Financial Times
26 January 2018

Covey, Steven
The 7 Habits of Highly Effective People
Simon and Schuster: Reprinted Edition
4 January 2004

Daily Telegraph
Antony Jenkins to staff: adopt new values or leave Barclays
17 January 2013

Damon, Professor William
The Path to Purpose
Free Press / Simon & Schuster NY
April 2009

Dennett, Daniel
Philosopher Daniel Dennett on AI, robots and religion
Financial Times - Interviewed by John Thornhill
3 March 2017

Delves Broughton, Philip
The path to power and how to use it
Financial Times
15 July 2013

Denning, Steven
The Age of Agile
AMACOM - the American Management Association
8 February 2018

Dermendzhiyska, Elitsa
Study by Eisenberger Naomi
Rejection kills
https://aeon.co/users/elitsa-dermendzhiyska
26 May 2019

Duhigg, Charles
What Google Learned from Its Quest to Build the Perfect Team
New York Times
25 February 2016

Edmondson, Amy C
The Fearless Organisation, 2019
John Wiley & Sons: Hoboken NJ, USA
Edmondson, Amy C

Psychological Safety and Learning Behaviour in
Work Teams
Administrative Science Quarterly, Vol. 44, No. 2,
June 1999, pp. 350-383
Johnson Graduate School of Management,
Cornell University

Eurich, Dr Tasha
What Self-Awareness Really Is (and How to Cultivate It)
Harvard Business Review
4 January 2018

Eby, Kate
Comprehensive Guide to the Agile Manifesto
Smartsheet.com
29 July 2016

Enright, Anne
The Gathering
Vintage Books: London
2008

Garvin, David A and Datar, Srikant M
Redesigning the MBA Curriculum: Implementation Challenges
Harvard Business School
2014

Gerber, Michael E
The E-Myth Revisited
Why Most Small Businesses Don't Work and What to Do About It
Harper Collins Inc: NY
14 October 2004

Gladwell, Malcolm
Blink: The Power of Thinking Without Thinking
Penguin Books: London
2 January 2006

Handy, Charles
The Second Curve
Random House Books: London
2015

Hamel, Gary
Can Big Firms Be Agile?
Steve Denning Senior Contributor
Forbes
27 November 2016

Helgesen, Sally
How to Create Meaning at Work When the Outcome Isn't Always Meaningful
Strategy + Business
14 January 2014

Herzberg, Frederick
https://en.wikipedia.org/wiki/Two-factor_theory

Hofstede, Professor Geert
Culture's Consequences: Comparing Values, Behaviours, Institutions and Organisations Across Nations
Sage Publications Inc. USA
2001

Jeffries, Stuart
Why did Andre Agassi hate tennis?
The Guardian
29 October 2009

Johnson, W. Brad and Smith, David G
Mentoring Someone with Imposter Syndrome
Harvard Business Review
22 February 2019

Katzenbach, Jon R and Smith, Douglas K
The Wisdom of Teams: Creating the High-Performance Organization
Harvard Business School Press
1993

Kellaway, Lucy
It is dangerous to feel passion for your work
Financial Times
8 June 2014

Magee, Patrick
VW set to unveil new strategy
Financial Times
2 April 2018

Mansoor, Sarfraz
S*tuds Terkel's Working – new jobs same need for meaning*
The Guardian
10 June 2017

Motoringpodcast.com
Follow up: ExEmployee feels misused by VW
https://www.motoringpodcast.com/
episodes/2017/12/5/episode-148-
6 December 2017

NPR Morning Edition
Volkswagen CEO: 'We Didn't Lie' About Emissions
13 January 2016

O' Neill, Professor Onora
TED talk: https://www.youtube.com/watch?v=1PNX6M_dVsk
25 September 2013

Pearl, David
Will There Be Donuts?
Harper Collins Publishers: London
2012

Pfeffer, Jeffrey
Dying for a Paycheck
Harper Business NY
2018

Pink, Daniel
Drive: The Surprising Truth About What Motivates Us
Riverhead Books NY
5 April 2011

Pinker, Steven
Enlightenment Now
The case for reason, science, humanism and progress
Penguin Books NY
2018

Pressman, Aaron
Inside T-Mobile's Big, Brash Comeback
15 February 2018

Rigby, Darrell K, Sutherland, Jeff and Takeuchi, Hirotaka
Embracing Agile
Harvard Business Review
May 2016

Russell, Oliver
Why corporate values should help avoid scandals
http://archives.oliverrussell.com/insights/blog/article/
corporate-values-volkswagen
22 October 2015

Ryan, Liz
How To Answer The 'Greatest Weakness' Question
Forbes
29 March 2017

Sills, Judith PhD
The Power of No
Psychology Today
5 November 2013
last reviewed on 9 June 2016

Schaffer, Robert
Successful Change Programs Begin with Results
Harvard Business Review January - February 1992

StrengthsQuest.com
About Clifton Strengths: *What is the difference between a talent and a strength?*
https://www.strengthsquest.com/help/general/143096/difference-talent-strength.aspx

Steiner, Susie
Five top regrets of the dying
The Guardian
1 February 2011

Taylor, Frederick Winslow
https://en.wikiquote.org/wiki/Frederick_Winslow_Taylor

The Cloverfield Paradox
Netflix (2018) (Germany) (video) (VOD)

Vaynerchuk, Gary
Advice for Millennials Entering Their First Job
26 May 2017

Wiersma, Bill and LaRussa, Tony
The Power of Professionalism: The Seven Mind-Sets that Drive Performance and Build Trust
Ravel
23 May 2011

About the Author

Alph Keogh is a learning and change consultant, coach, facilitator and speaker. He has more than 25 years' experience in the area of international executive education and leadership development. He has worked extensively in the areas of employee onboarding and engagement, career transition, change, leadership purpose and coaching. Recognised as possessing outstanding conceptual, design and delivery skills he works across a variety of industries including Manufacturing, Energy, Aviation, Shipping, Financial and Legal Services, FMCG and Life Sciences.

He has led executive programmes and delivered keynotes in more than 40 countries worldwide. He is a renowned storyteller and enjoys mixing science and stories as a means of making messages both compelling and memorable. He holds a BSc in Psychology from the University of London and a Masters in Intelligent Knowledge Based Systems from the Polytechnic of the South Bank in London. He is the Managing Director of Business Learning Solutions GmbH and YourOnBoard.com based in Munich, Germany and Dublin, Ireland.

You can reach him at alph.keogh@bizlernsol.com

Printed in Poland
by Amazon Fulfillment
Poland Sp. z o.o., Wrocław

66053477R00114